halloween woodcarving

halloween woodcarving

by Cyndi Joslyn

Fox Chapel Publishing
1970 Broad Street • East Petersburg, PA 17520
www.FoxChapelPublishing.com

© 2008 by Fox Chapel Publishing Company, Inc.

Halloween Woodcarving is an original work, first published in 2007 by Fox Chapel Publishing Company, Inc. The patterns contained herein are copyrighted by the author. Readers may make copies of these patterns for personal use. The patterns themselves, however, are not to be duplicated for resale or distribution under any circumstances. Any such copying is a violation of copyright law.

ISBN 978-1-56523-289-1

Cover photography by Greg Heisey

Publisher's Cataloging-in-Publication Data

Joslyn-Carhart, Cyndi.
    Halloween woodcarving / by Cyndi Joslyn. -- East Petersburg, PA :
Fox Chapel Publishing, c2008.
        p. : col. ill. ; cm.
        ISBN: 978-1-56523-289-1

        1. Wood-carving--Patterns. 2. Wood-carved figurines--Patterns.
    3. Halloween decorations--Patterns. I. Title.

TT199.7 .J674 2008
745.594/1646--dc22   0803

To learn more about the other great books from
Fox Chapel Publishing, or to find a retailer near you,
call toll-free 1-800-457-9112 or visit us at *www.FoxChapelPublishing.com*.

Note to Authors: We are always looking for talented
authors to write new books in our area of woodworking, design,
and related crafts. Please send a brief letter describing your idea to
Peg Couch, Acquisition Editor, 1970 Broad Street, East Petersburg, PA 17520.

Printed in China
10 9 8 7 6 5 4 3 2 1

Because carving wood and other materials inherently includes the risk of injury and damage, this book cannot guarantee that creating the projects in this book is safe for everyone. For this reason, this book is sold without warranties or guarantees of any kind, expressed or implied, and the publisher and the author disclaim any liability for any injuries, losses, or damages caused in any way by the content of this book or the reader's use of the tools needed to complete the projects presented here. The publisher and the author urge all carvers to thoroughly review each project and to understand the use of all tools before beginning any project.

about the author

Cyndi Joslyn is a professional woodcarver with flair for handcarved folk art figures. Her work is sold through several exclusive shops and galleries across the country. Joslyn also has designed and carved more than two dozen ornaments and figurines for Big Sky Carvers, a Montana company that produces and distributes resin-cast ornaments of her original handcarved designs.

In the 1990s, Joslyn took part in a volunteer effort to produce one of the first handcarved carousels created since the 1930s. The collection of 38 carved ponies and two chariots, completed in 1995 in Missoula, Montana, drew national attention. Her outstanding talent earned Joslyn the distinction of being the only woman "head carver" on the project.

Joslyn is also an experienced author. Joslyn's works have appeared in *Woodcarving Illustrated* and *Woodworking for Women*. Joslyn is the author of: *North Woods Nativity*, featuring step-by-step directions on how to carve a sixteen-piece woodland nativity set; *Carving Santas from Around the World*, an easy-to-understand handbook that guides beginners through 15 Santa carvings based on figures from around the globe; and *Easy Woodcarving*, which includes simple skill-building exercises and projects for beginners.

A woodcarving teacher for the past 17 years, Joslyn loves to share her passion with others. She works tirelessly to perpetuate the art by encouraging beginners and helping to instill in them a love of carving.

To learn more about Joslyn, visit her Website at *www.cyndijoslyn.com*.

contents

introduction

If you've read any of my other books, you know one of my main goals is to make learning to carve easy. When I first started carving, I found the whole process intimidating. Finding answers to questions on my own and working through any frustrations fueled my desire to help new carvers so no one had to struggle for information as I did.

To that end, you'll find everything you need on the pages of this book to get you started in carving, including some fun Halloween projects into which you may jump once you understand the basics. We'll go over the use and care of the basic tools, the pros and cons of different types of wood, general carving information, basic techniques, guidelines and safety instructions, the different types of finishes, and pattern making and transfer techniques. As you work through the basic carving techniques and the projects in this book, you'll notice my carving patterns and techniques come from what I call block carving. That is, I often start with a block of wood and carve it into something, rather than starting with preformed shapes. I believe the block carving approach allows carvers to be more creative and doesn't lock them into someone else's idea of what the project should be. You'll also see my patterns are more similar to patterns crafters use, unlike traditional carving patterns, which often show only an outline of the finished project.

More than anything, I hope this book will give you confidence to create your own designs and allow you to truly enjoy the craft of carving.

—Cyndi Joslyn

getting started

Planning out your carving space and understanding your tools are the first steps toward an enjoyable carving experience. Many new carvers want to skip these steps entirely, but I truly believe a little planning and some basic knowledge go a long way.

Some of the first things we'll discuss are the different types of tools and their functions. Having a solid understanding of what each tool does, how to use it, and when to use it will make the actual carving process much easier.

You'll also learn sharp tools are essential. Many beginning carvers become frustrated quickly because they find removing wood to be so difficult. Often, a dull knife is the culprit, and the difficulty can be overcome by knowing a bit about tuning up your tools.

Safety equipment is just as important as tools, and we'll cover them as well. Keeping yourself safe and injury-free is an all-important part of enjoying carving.

I'll also provide some information on selecting wood and using finishes. Understanding both areas will round out your knowledge, help you quickly select the items you need, and allow you to complete your projects.

setting up your work space

It doesn't take a huge shop and thousands of dollars of equipment to begin a very satisfying experience in woodcarving. You don't even need a space where you can permanently set up shop, so to speak. The kitchen table or space in an existing craft room is an adequate carving space for beginning carvers. Just make sure you have a work surface of about 18" x 32".

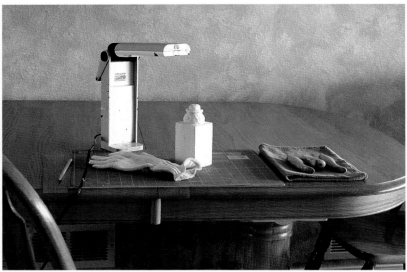

The simplest setup. Permanent space is not necessary. A little room at the kitchen table is all the space you need to set up shop.

Basic carving space. My carving space: I find wire shelves and movable storage drawers hold all of my supplies conveniently within arm's reach.

You'll also need a place to store your tools and projects when you are not carving. All of your tools, equipment, supplies, and wood should easily fit in a large plastic container. A shop vacuum, stored in a corner or under a table, makes cleanup a breeze.

lighting

Good lighting is important. You must be able to clearly and without shadows see the wood and where you are cutting. I use a full-spectrum, nonglare natural light, such as an Ott-Lite, which is commonly used by quilters and crafters. A full-spectrum light allows me to see in greater detail. The one in the photos at left is a compact version that folds for storage, if desired.

self-healing mat

If you are carving on a kitchen or dining room table, a self-healing mat, like the Olfa one pictured in the top left photo, provides plenty of protection for your tabletop in case of an occasional slip. Olfa does make a translucent 3 mm mat that is twice as thick as its standard green mat and is specifically designed for use with heavy-duty cutters and craft knives.

seating

Another item to consider, especially if you do a lot of carving, is a comfortable chair. I experimented with several before I found one I really liked. I use an ergonomic office chair with a variety of adjustments for height, lumbar support, etc. Although it is certainly not a required item, it is something your body will truly appreciate if you find yourself doing a lot of carving.

understanding basic carving tools

There are literally hundreds of carving tools with very specific purposes; however, I have learned working with so many tools can be difficult and time-consuming. You spend a lot of time trying to locate one particular tool and then more time moving from one tool to another. From a production standpoint, it is not very efficient. It also can get quite expensive.

The more you can get done with one tool, the better off you will be. I have 35 to 45 different tools right now, but the ones I use repeatedly are those I recommend as the four basic tools: a bench knife, a detail knife, a #3 22-mm (⅞") gouge or a #3 16-mm (⅝") gouge, and a 1-mm V-tool.

Before you go out and buy any tools, take a look at the following information about the different types of carving tools. Understanding the basic types and their functions will allow you to customize your tool set to suit the kinds of projects that you prefer.

One word of caution: Though it may be enticing, resist the urge to buy inexpensive sets of carving tools. They are likely to chip and break more easily and need to be replaced more often, whereas a few well-selected, quality carving tools that are well maintained will serve you for years. Quality tools stay sharper longer, and sharp tools are the foundation of a comfortable, quality carving experience. I have tools I've been using every day for fifteen years, and they are still in good shape. Good tools are lifelong companions, so do not skimp on quality.

Due to the increasing popularity of hand carving, tools and supplies are more readily available today through quality craft stores, mail-order companies, and the Internet. I buy most of what I need online, where I can research and study each product. You can make more educated decisions about which tools are right for you by using online resources and reading the following tool section.

knives

Knives are used to score wood, to round and shape, and to carve and clean up details. Any carving knives should have comfortable handles and blades made of hardened and tempered high-carbon steel. Look for tools honed by the manufacturer. Honing means the tools have been factory sharpened and polished, and are ready to use.

Knives are generally identified by type, and each type of knife varies in its characteristics depending on the manufacturer. Regardless of the type of knife you are using, knives with blades that are 1½" long and under are good choices for the beginning carver. Anything longer than 1½" can be intimidating and harder to control.

To hold a knife, place the handle in the palm of your hand with the blade going in the same direction as your thumb, and then wrap all four fingers around the handle. This is called an overhand grip. Your thumb provides the pushing action against the back of the blade or helps to hold the wood in place.

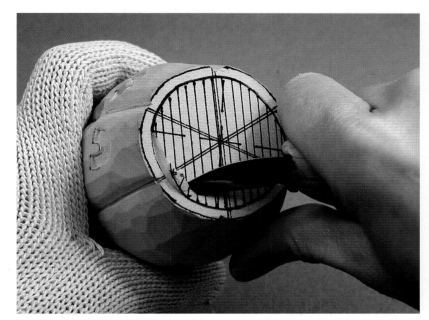

Overhand grip with a knife. Hold the handle of the knife in the palm of your hand. The blade goes the same direction as your thumb, and all four fingers should wrap around the handle. Note that my thumb stays out of the way.

knives you should know

Here, we will take a brief look at some of the common types of knives. The bench knife and the detail knife are often used to complete the projects in this book.

Bench knife. The bench knife has a sturdy blade and is used for scoring, rounding, and shaping.

Detail knife. Delicate details are carved with the thin, sharp-tipped blade of a detail knife.

Skew knife. The 45-degree angle of this knife blade creates the geometric shapes associated with chip carving.

bench knife: The foundation knife of your tool collection. It generally has a wider blade than most other types of knives. Because of its sturdy blade, a good amount of pressure can be applied to deeply score wood with this knife. It can also be used for rounding and for some preliminary shaping.

detail knife: Perfect for getting into areas that are too small to access with a bench knife because it has a much thinner blade that comes to a very fine point. It is used to remove wood in tight areas and to carve delicate details. The tip is very thin, so extra care must be taken when carving with it. Apply too much pressure, and the tip will break off.

skew knife: Specialty knife used to create the wonderful triangular-shaped cuts that denote chip carvings, which entail cutting a series of free-form or geometric patterns on flat pieces of wood. The skew knife has a short, flat edge honed to a 45-degree angle to create the accent wedge of the chip-carved triangle.

The skew knife, also called the stabbing knife, can be held with an overhand grip (like a dagger) or with an underhand grip, just as you would hold a pencil.

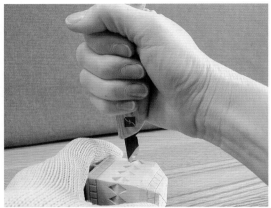

Overhand grip with the skew knife. Hold the skew knife just as you would hold a dagger.

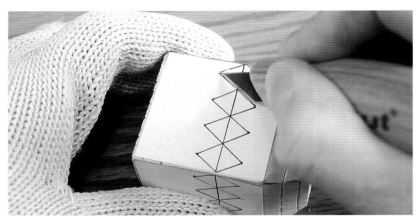

Underhand grip with the skew knife. To use the underhand grip, hold the skew knife as you would hold a pencil. While this grip of the skew knife is somewhat untraditional, I have found it to be the most effective method for beginning chip carvings.

gouges

Gouges are shaped pieces of sharpened metal that are attached to wooden handles. Typically, a gouge has only one beveled edge. Gouges are used to shape wooden surfaces and create texture in carvings. They are identified by the size, or width, of the blade, the curvature of the blade, and the style of the tool.

The degree of curvature in a gouge is known as its sweep. The sweep of a gouge is identified by a number. Each manufacturer has its own system for classifying the degree of this curvature. In general, a low sweep number indicates a shallow curve and a higher number indicates a deeper curve. The deeper-curved tools remove more wood and are good for roughing out. The deeper the curve, the more texture is created in the wood.

Another consideration in gouge selection is blade length. Blade length determines how many times a gouge can be sharpened. Each time a tool is sharpened, a tiny portion of its metal edge is ground away. A gouge with a blade length of 2" to 4" can be sharpened many more times than one whose tempered end is only ½".

To hold a gouge, place the handle of the gouge across the palm of your hand with the blade pointing away from your thumb; then, wrap all four fingers around the handle, and close your thumb on top of your fingers, almost as if you were holding an ice pick. Of course, you'll be using a controlled cutting motion, not a quick stabbing motion, when you are carving!

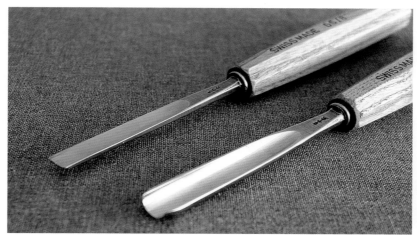

Sweep. The tool on the left is a gouge with a #5 sweep, whereas the tool on the right is a #9. The sweep indicates the curvature of the blade.

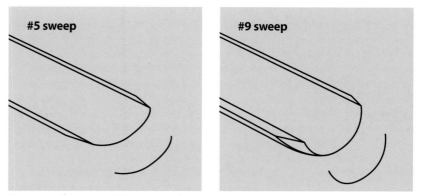

Sweep and texture. The sweep of a gouge determines the texture it leaves in wood. Higher-numbered gouges remove more wood and create deeper texture.

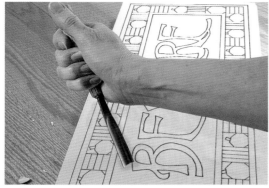

Grip. To hold a gouge, place the handle across the palm of your hand, and wrap all four fingers around the handle, closing your thumb on top of your fingers.

Blade length. The price of the tool on the top is almost twice that of the tool on the bottom. However, its functional life is many times greater because of the length of its blade, which makes it a very good value—even at a higher price.

common gouge blade sizes and sweeps

Most gouges of any given sweep come in a variety of blade sizes. For example, a gouge with a #3 sweep might be available in blades that are anywhere from 6 to 20 mm wide. We'll look at a few different gouges, focusing mostly on sweep, because it is the sweep that primarily determines the shape of the tool.

I also will say a few words about blade width.

gouges: Your normal gouge is any gouge with a sweep between #1 and #11. The tools have anywhere from no curve to an extreme U-shaped blade. Gouges come in a variety of blade widths ranging from .5 to 60 mm.

The #3 22 mm (⅞") and the #3 16 mm (⅝") gouges I recommend as basic tools have only slight sweeps so they will remove smaller amounts of wood, making them easy to manage for a beginner. I have found this tool size range to be very versatile.

chisels and skews: Chisels and skews are gouges that have no sweep. They are completely flat at the cutting edge, but a chisel's edge is straight and a skew's edge is angled, or skewed. Chisels work well to outline projects, such as the Beware Sign on page 108. Skews are handy for getting into tight-

V-tools. V-tools form a V-shaped trench and are especially useful for creating fur and hair textures.

angled places, such as when removing wood from inside the pumpkins' features on page 61. Chisels are also referred to as #1 sweep. I hold the skew as I would any other gouge.

V-tools: A V-tool is a useful specialty gouge. Its sweep is in the shape of a V, and its function is to carve an angled trench with straight sides and a V-shaped bottom edge in one carved stroke. V-tools are very handy for carving outlines and cleaning up edges of recessed wood and are also used to create a variety of textures—from crosshatching and scrollwork to the textures of fur and hair. Larger V-tools can be used with a mallet.

V-tools are a little more complicated when it comes to deciphering their descriptions. Some manufacturers describe their tools in degrees, such as 45, 60, and 90. A 45-degree V-tool will give you a narrower trench, and the trench will appear darker in color. A 90-degree V-tool will give you a wider trench that will appear lighter in color. Swiss tools use numbers to designate their degree of angle. For example, #15 is 45 degrees, #12 is 60 degrees, and #13 is 90 degrees.

A V-tool can be held like a knife or like a gouge, depending on the area you want to carve.

common gouge styles

In addition to their designations by blade size and sweep, gouges can also be broken down by style. Differences in handles, overall size, and intended use define the categories.

Chisel and skew. The gouge with the flat head is called a chisel (left). A flat chisel with an angled edge is called a skew (not to be confused with the skew knife).

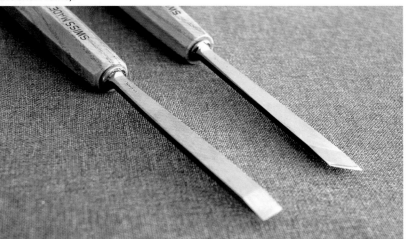

traditional tools: Traditional carving gouges are 9½" to 11" long with blade lengths of 3½" to 4". They have octagonal wooden handles from ¾" to 1" in diameter. Traditional tools are also available in widths up to 60 millimeters. These tools, especially the larger widths, are frequently used with the aid of a carving mallet.

palm tools: Palm tools are gouges with shorter, rounded handles specially designed to conform to the inside curvature of your palm. Rather than being tapped with a mallet, palm tools are powered by direct pressure from the hand.

intermediate tools: Intermediate tools are gouges that are approximately 8" long with blades that range from 2" to 2¼". The handles are ⅝" in diameter. The versatile tools can be used with or without a mallet.

mallets

A mallet is used to tap a gouge or a chisel into the wood. There are several different styles. Some are flat-faced squares or rectangles, but the turned mallet is the one most often associated with carving. A turned mallet has a smooth, round surface that evenly impacts the handle of the tool regardless of what part of the mallet strikes the handle. This feature makes the turned mallet good for a beginning woodcarver.

Mallets come in different weights, usually 12 to 36 ounces. Lighter mallets are used with small-diameter gouges; heavier mallets are used with larger carving tools. It is the weight of the mallet, not the arm swing behind it, that drives the gouge through the wood.

Mallets are tapped, not swung. Never use steel hammers on your gouges because they will quickly damage the handles. I prefer the newer high-tech version of the turned mallet with a urethane head because it is quieter with less vibration and is gentler on tool handles.

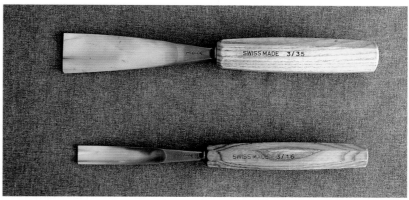

Wide blades. Gouges with wide blades are commonly used with a mallet.

Palm tools. Palm tools are about 4½" long, with handles that fit the inside surface of your hand.

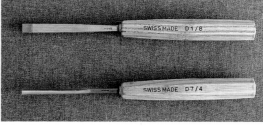

Intermediate tools. Intermediate tools can be used with or without a mallet.

Mallet use. This photo shows how to properly hold a mallet. A 12- to 18-ounce turned mallet is a good choice for a beginning carver.

choosing your first tools

I have three tools I use to do 80 percent of my carving—a bench knife, a detail knife, and a #3 22 mm (⅞") gouge. There are several other tools that I have used on the projects in this book that are very handy for specialized applications.

four basic tools

What it looks like	What it is	Why you need it	Where you use it
	Bench knife	To score wood and round preliminary shapes	
	Detail knife	To carve in tight areas where a bench knife won't reach and carve details	
	#3 16 mm (⅝") gouge (shallow sweep)*	To rough out preliminary shapes	
	1 mm V-tool	To incise fine lines	

* The #3 16 mm (⅝") gouge and the #3 22 mm (⅞") gouge are interchangeable. For the beginning carver, only one is required.

additional tools

What it looks like	What it is	Why you need it	Where you use it
	#3 22 mm (⅞") gouge (shallow sweep)*	To remove large amounts of wood and rough out preliminary shapes	
	#5 3 mm (⅛") gouge (medium sweep)	To remove wood and add texture in small areas	
	#8 7 mm gouge	To add character lines	
	#9 5 mm gouge	To add texture and curve to small areas	
	#9 10 mm gouge	To carve deeply curved trenches	
	#11 1 mm gouge	To add high-relief fine detail	
	#11 3 mm (⅛") gouge	To carve a uniformly round hole	

sharpening tools

You should no more carve with a dull tool than you would shave with a dull razor. In both cases, the result will be much the same—nicks and scrapes. The sharper and more highly polished the surface of the knife, the more easily it slides through wood. Once a blade gets dull, you need to use more force to push it through the wood, and the knife catches and snags.

If you choose to sharpen your tools yourself, I suggest you invest in the proper equipment and a good book or DVD on how to sharpen tools. Because tool sharpening is an art unto itself and entire books have been written just on sharpening, I will not be covering that process here. Sharpening requires patience and practice, and you may go through many good tools before you perfect it.

If you choose not to sharpen your own tools, then find someone in your area who can do it for you. Be sure to look for someone who has experience in sharpening *carving* tools. Many carving clubs have someone who really enjoys the art of tool sharpening, and, for a very minimal price, that person can keep your tools in tip-top shape. Woodworking stores are also a good resource for finding people who sharpen tools.

strops

Even if you decide not to sharpen your tools yourself, you will want to have the tools necessary to strop all of your blades. Stropping, or honing, is a process used to regularly polish a tool's edge. The goal of stropping is to maintain the sharpness of the tool and postpone the actual sharpening process for as long as possible because, each time you sharpen a tool, you grind away a portion of its metal edge, thus reducing its life span.

If you do not strop your tools, you will start knocking the points off knives and end up shredding your wood as you carve. Carving without stropping is not efficient because carving turns into more of a grating process than a smooth, gliding process.

You can purchase a strop at most carving supply stores or online. Listed on page 11 are the different types of strops and their uses. You also can make your own strop fairly easily because it is basically a piece of leather on a stick (see "Make Your Own Strop," below).

Make Your Own Strop

You will need a piece of wood about 2" wide x ½" thick x 12" long. Cut a piece of leather—almost any type will work—to fit the lower portion of the wood, leaving the upper portion for a handle. I like to use tooling leather, which I get from my local cobbler or saddle maker. It is smooth on one side, rough on the other side, and approximately ³⁄₁₆" thick. A thicker piece of leather adds to the durability of the strop. Glue the leather onto the strop with some contact cement, and you're good to go.

A lot of times you will see leather on both sides of a strop. One side will have the rough side of the leather out, and the other side will have the smooth side out. In stropping, you move from the rough side, which takes off more material, over to the smoother side, which refines the whole process.

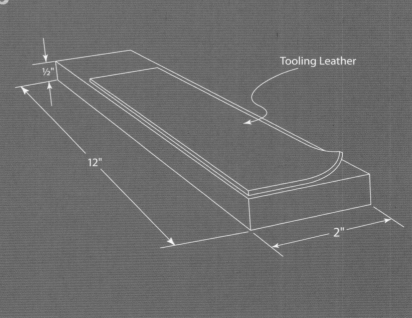

Tooling Leather

½"

12"

2"

types of strops

There are a variety of strops available, from simple strops that have general uses, to specialty strops designed to help you hone specific tools. A brief overview of some of the most common types follows.

Many people use honing compound in conjunction with their strops. Honing compound helps enhance and speed up the polishing process. The compound, an abrasive powder that comes in a variety of forms, can be used with any of these strops.

basic strop: A strop is a length of leather fastened to a wooden handle. Many strops are two sided: The rough side of the leather faces out on one side; the smooth side faces out on the other side. Basic strops are perfect for knives. Because gouges and V-tools have curved or angled interior surfaces, they require a different type of strop.

Butz strop: A Butz strop has flat surfaces for stropping knives, as well as a curved edge for stropping the inside surfaces of gouges and an angled edge for stropping the inside surfaces of V-tools. While the Butz strop is a good choice, it is more expensive than the basic strop.

slip strop: A two-sided slip strop is made of wood and includes a number of curved and angled profiles to facilitate polishing the inside surfaces of a variety of gouges. The slip strop requires honing compound. Simply apply a honing compound to the shaped wooden surfaces and strop the tools over those surfaces. A slip strop also has two smaller leather strips for stropping. The slip strop is versatile and economically priced.

Basic strop. A simple strop is perfect for stropping knives.

Butz strop. The curved and angled sides sharpen gouges and V-tools. Use the flat surface to sharpen knives.

Slip strop. The strop's two sides include a variety of surfaces for stropping gouges, V-tools, and knives.

safety equipment

Because carvers deal with razor-sharp tools, steps must be taken to protect both the tools and the carver. There are supplies you can purchase or make that help you play it safe. Tool rolls and carving aprons are by no means new to the art of carving, but are very necessary, and you should invest in them up front.

Many commercially made items are available, ranging in price, style, and material. I have designed patterns for a tool roll and a carving apron with the beginner in mind. These exclusive designs, shown in the photos below, are relatively easy and inexpensive to make and highly effective at protecting the carver and the tools. Other items you should consider purchasing are a Kevlar glove and thumb guards. We will discuss the importance of each of these safety items.

Tool roll. This well-designed tool roll snugly contains tools in an easy-to-transport bundle. You can easily make a tool roll like this to protect your tools (and you) from accidental damage.

Carving apron. This simple apron features a removable leather patch and provides lightweight, breathable, dye-free protection while carving.

tool roll

You only have to drop your tool on a hard surface once—or slice a finger reaching for a tool—to realize the value of a tool roll. It is very disheartening to be all ready to jump right into a carving project only to pick up a chipped knife or, worse, to cut yourself. Then, you are back to square one. If you go through all of the trouble to sharpen and hone your tools, you do not want them dropping out of a bag onto the floor or banging against each other in a shoebox.

A well-designed tool roll is necessary to protect your tools and you. I say "well-designed" because not all tool rolls are constructed with a flap that pulls down over the tops of the tools and keeps them from slipping out of the roll. I had difficulty finding one like that, so I settled for one without a flap for a while.

carving apron

Some people say I am a bit of a samurai carver, which is probably true. I think a lot of women carvers tend to carve toward themselves because they do get better leverage that way. But I got tired of all the little holes in my shirts from where I got a little too close. That is where the carving apron comes in.

A carving apron is designed to protect your torso and lap from those little mishaps. Traditionally, these aprons have been all leather and cover you from your neck to your knees. Leather aprons provide the protection you need, but tend to be very hot and cumbersome. Often the leather is dyed, and the dye comes off on everything, including your carvings.

I tried many different types of aprons until finally coming up with my own solution—a canvas apron with a removable leather patch just big enough to offer the right protection. I designed it so the leather patch is attached to the apron with Velcro and can be removed. You can take off the leather patch for laundering or replace it when you happen to carve through it too often. From a functionality standpoint, the apron is more comfortable and convenient, while at the same time offering you the protection you need. But whether you choose to buy one or make your own, you should not attempt to carve without a protective apron.

Kevlar glove

The most significant thing you can do to carve safely is to carve with sharp tools. That's because sharp tools move more easily through wood, using less force. However, they can be dangerous, and mishaps do occur. I've had many nicks and scrapes on my hands but nothing serious because I take the proper precautions—like wearing a Kevlar-reinforced carving glove.

Kevlar gloves are actually the gloves that meat cutters use. They are worn on the hand that does not hold the knife and are wonderfully cut resistant. The Kevlar glove is not puncture resistant. If you take your detail knife and stab your glove, it will go through. But if, in the course of carving, you slip and the knife blade impacts the glove, it will deflect the blow and keep your hand and fingers safe.

You can find Kevlar gloves at a carving supply store or order directly online.

thumb guard

Although I don't use one, some people also wear a thumb guard for additional safety on the hand that holds the knife. Thumb guards come in many different variations but usually consist of a piece of leather attached to a piece of elastic that slips down over your thumb. You can also purchase reinforced self-sticking thumb and finger tape to wrap your fingers for further protection.

A thumb guard can be good for beginners just getting used to handling carving tools. If you use a thumb guard, be sure it fits snugly down over your thumb. If it does not fit tight, it is likely to slip and just be in the way.

health and focus

Never attempt carving while you are on medication that might affect your vision or coordination. And never carve when you are overtired, because this will lead to mishaps. Woodcarving requires total focus and concentration, and anything that detracts from that is inadvisable. Perhaps I overdo the safety warnings, but I believe it is very important. Using good common sense will help keep carving a safe, relaxing, and enjoyable pursuit.

Kevlar glove. A Kevlar-reinforced carving glove will protect your hand from nicks and cuts during your carving sessions. However, remember Kevlar gloves are not puncture resistant!

selecting wood

Wood to the carver is like clay to the potter, fabric to the quilter, or a canvas to the painter. It is the medium through which you express your art. For that reason, I suggest you become familiar with the different types of woods available to woodcarvers and experiment with them until you find the wood that suit your specific needs and style.

Most woods fall into two categories: hard and soft. A simple way to learn the difference is to remember hardwood comes from trees

Basswood. Perfect for beginners, this wood comes from linden trees and is sometimes called lime wood. Although classified as a hardwood, this pale, cream-colored wood is one of the softer hardwoods. It has a fine texture and a tight, even grain with very few knots or blemishes, and it holds details well.

Sugar pine. Classified as a softwood, sugar pine is another acceptable, easy-to-carve wood for beginners. However, your tools must be razor sharp, or you run the risk of mushing up the details. For that reason, softer woods require tools with a longer bevel than those used on hardwoods. So unless you plan to have two separate sets of tools, it is best to focus on one wood type or the other, at least in the beginning.

Butternut. This wood is another interesting option for beginners. Although classified as a hardwood, it is considered to be of medium hardness with a medium-coarse texture and a beautiful grain pattern. Its coloration runs from cream to reddish brown.

with leaves that drop during the winter, such as maple, oak, walnut, and pecan. Softwood comes from trees that do not have leaves, but rather needles, such as pine and fir. Within each category, there are many subcategories or degrees of hardness. For example, walnut and butternut are both hardwoods, but walnut is harder than butternut, making it more challenging to carve.

You might think the softer the wood, the better it is for carving, but that is only true to an extent. Some softwoods, such as balsa, are so soft they often crush when you try to carve them and do not retain any detail. Pine is a softwood that's a little harder than balsa. Because of that, it might be an acceptable wood, but carving pine requires a different angle on your tools, and the tools must be very sharp so you don't mush up a face or detail. I recommend using basswood for your first project. The photos and information in this section will help you choose wood for your projects.

wood grain

In choosing wood, it is important to consider the grain of a particular piece of wood. Why? Because every time you carve across it, you run the risk of wood chipping off your carving, and that is certainly not what you want. So before you begin your carving project, pay attention to which way the grain is running. The wood grain always runs the length of the wood.

purchasing wood

You can purchase blocks of wood for carving that have already been processed and refined. They are planed and cut into blocks of specific sizes and then air- or kiln-dried. The blocks of wood are available on the Internet or locally through carving supply stores and specialty wood stores that sell carving wood. If you are not sure what you need, spend some time browsing through catalogs or go online to see what is available. The Internet is a valuable resource both in learning what is available to beginning carvers and for ordering wood.

Most of my experience has been in buying carving wood, so your experience may be slightly different if you are buying wood through a construction lumber dealer. For me, basswood purchased from a lumberyard has not been great to carve. I recommend buying wood from a source specializing in carving wood.

Wood is usually sold by the board foot. Whether you purchase your wood online, through a catalog store, or at a lumberyard, make sure you get what you want by always using this wood measurement equation:

Thickness x Width x Length

The first measurement given in ordering wood is the thickness of the wood in inches (2-inch stock refers to wood that is 2 inches thick). The second measurement given is the width of the wood in inches. The final measurement is the length of the wood in inches.

One board foot is 1" thick x 12" wide x 12" long. To determine board feet, multiply length (in inches) by width (in inches). Multiply that number by the thickness of the board (in inches), and then divide by 144, which is the number of square inches in one board foot.

Example:

6 (length) x 14 (width) = 84

84 x 2 (thickness) = 168

168 ÷ 144 (number of square inches in one board foot) = 1.167 board feet

Board feet. One board foot equals 1" thick x 12"

Carving with the grain. To determine the grain of the wood, test carve on the edge of a block. When you are carving with the grain, the knife or gouge will move easily through the wood and produce little wood curls and smooth facets. The tool will naturally rise back up to the surface of the wood. Carving against the grain will feel as if your tool is being pulled deeper into the wood. Experiment with a couple of pieces of wood, and you will be able to determine the grain of the wood easily. Remember, the grain may change within any particular block.

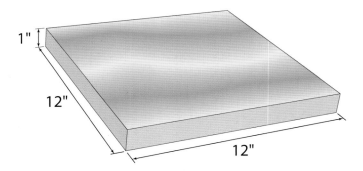

Board feet. One board foot equals 1" thick x 12" wide x 12" long.

found wood

You may want to gather your carving materials straight from Mother Nature. It's fun and soothing to the soul to get out there and scavenge around in the great outdoors looking for the perfect piece of wood. With any luck, you might locate some diamond willow branches or a sturdy piece of cottonwood bark or a curiously shaped cypress knee. All of these would make wonderful carvings. But they do require extra preparation on your part to remove (or peel) bark, clean them, and dry them.

Found woods can be very enjoyable to carve, but keep in mind they all contain sand and grit that remain even after their initial cleaning. The sand and grit will require a bit more maintenance on your part because your tools will dull more quickly. Still, the emotional rewards of carving that special piece of wood you found yourself may be worth the extra effort. If you like the look of found wood, but don't want to find it yourself, you may find it for sale on an Internet site.

cutouts and boxes

With the growing popularity of what craft stores are calling wood décor, it is now easier to find pre-made boxes and precut shapes. With a little investigating, you can find many of the products are now available in basswood. Pre-made boxes come in all sorts of shapes and sizes—from plain old rectangles to attractive hearts and octagons. Precut shapes, often called cutouts, come in just about any shape you can imagine.

If you have a scroll saw, you can cut these shapes on your own. If not, you can purchase them to use in your carving or you might seek out a woodcarving or scroll sawing group for someone who is willing to saw up whatever shapes you need. Be sure to ask what type of wood the boxes and cutouts are made from. You'll want to use only those made from real wood, not plywood or pressed wood.

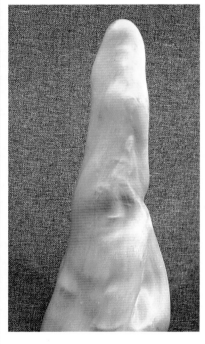

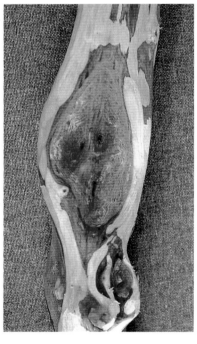

Found wood. Found wood, like this cypress knee, diamond willow branch, and section of cottonwood bark, is relatively easy to locate and fun to carve, despite the extra effort required to prepare it for carving.

painting and finishing supplies

I may not know exactly how I want to finish a piece until I am actually done carving it. As a result, I like to have a variety of finishing supplies on hand so I'll have everything I need to finish it.

In this section, we'll go over some different finishing supplies so you can learn some of the options. Following is a basic list of the items I use to finish my carvings. Of course, if you decide you like only a few types of finishes, you don't need to have all of these items on hand.

acrylic paint: Available in a variety of colors and are readily available in carving supply and craft supply stores. They are quick drying and are easily blended with other colors or thinned with water. I like the 2-ounce bottles of acrylic paint and almost exclusively use Delta Ceramcoat paints. A 6" x 6" piece of folded wax paper serves as my palette.

water-based satin varnish: Great for woods with appealing grain patterns, water-based satin varnish also can be used over a painted carving. Varnish can be found at all paint, hardware, and craft stores. Be sure to look for a satin finish; you don't want your finished piece to be too glossy. The water-based type makes for easier cleanup.

wood stain: Stains come in a variety of finishes—oak, maple, walnut, cherry, and pine, for example—and are perfect for accentuating woods with visible grain patterns. Wood stains can be found wherever hardware and paint supplies are sold.

Danish oil: Danish oil stains, seals, and protects in a one-step process. The finish penetrates and hardens in the wood, as opposed to sitting on top of it, and creates the look of a hand-rubbed finish. Always wear rubber gloves when working with Danish oil because it contains resins that should not be absorbed into the skin.

Finishing supplies.
Having a variety of painting and finishing supplies on hand gives you options when you are ready to finish a carving.

boiled linseed oil: An oil finish is ideal for showing off the wood grain. Boiled linseed oil is easy to use and creates a wonderful result. Be sure to read the safety precautions on the product package when using it.

paste wax: Gives a hard, durable finish to carvings with a natural finish. Paste wax can be used as a final finish to any previously applied painting or finishing technique.

antiquing medium and retarder: There are many extender and retarder products on the market. I like to use Jo Sonja's retarder and mix it with equal parts of any acrylic paint to create an antiquing mixture. The mixture is painted on and quickly wiped off with a soft, dry cloth until the desired effect is achieved.

disposable foam brushes: Inexpensive brushes are great for applying finishes that would ruin your good paintbrushes, such as stain.

paintbrushes: For acrylic paint, I recommend shader brushes in sizes 2, 6, and 8, such as Loew-Cornell Series #4300, and a liner brush in size 1, such as Loew-Cornell Series #4050. For varnishing, I use a ¾" wash brush from the Loew-Cornell Series #4550. Any old, worn-out brush or a cloth will work well for applying oil. It is important to use a good-quality paintbrush because a wonderful carving can be ruined when poorly painted.

clean cloths: Rags are used for applying

finishes. Old, worn-out T-shirts can be great for applying antiquing and oil finishes. White T-shirts are best; I have had some problems with colored fuzz when using colored T-shirts.

rubber gloves: I only wear rubber gloves when I do oil finishes or work with stain. Oil finishes are messy, and Danish oil products contain resins you do not want absorbed into your body. I prefer latex gloves to the heavy rubber ones you would wear to wash dishes. Latex gloves are thin and allow you to maintain your dexterity while wearing them.

cheesecloth: Cheesecloth is a great tool for getting an even coat of paste wax on a carving.

other supplies

Carving is not just my passion—it's my business. That's why I want to make it as efficient and streamlined as possible. When I start a piece, I like to be sure I have everything I need at the outset so I can complete it without running around looking for additional items I may need to get the job done.

In the safety section, I listed some things that would help ensure a comfortable, safe carving experience. The next items are additional supplies you may want to keep on hand to assist with your carving projects. Many of them are common items you may already have around the house. I suggest you collect them and keep them in one central location so you know where they are when you need them.

12" flexible ruler: Measuring takes the guesswork out of proportions and lengths. My favorite measuring instrument is a clear 2-inch-wide sewing ruler. Because it is clear, you can see exactly what you are measuring underneath.

calipers: Calipers work well for measuring thickness at various points on a carving that would be difficult to measure using conventional rulers.

pencil: I use a pencil in every carving project to draw the reference and pattern lines on each block of wood. A common No. 2 pencil works well.

graphite paper: Used to transfer a pattern to the block of wood. Graphite paper can be found in stationery or craft supply stores.

tissue paper: Keep a supply of tissue paper on hand if you choose to trace patterns from the book. You may find it easier to photocopy the patterns.

scissors: In addition to being generally handy, scissors are particularly useful for cutting out gridded template patterns.

quick-grip all-purpose adhesive: I much prefer this type of glue to typical wood glue. Quick-grip glue, such as the type from Beacon Adhesives, typically dries clear and bonds in about 15 minutes.

wood repair epoxy putty: Everybody makes an occasional mistake. Wood repair epoxy putty is very handy for places where I might not have carved as well as I had hoped. It fills in unwanted gouges, low spots, or gaps in blocks. It allows one more opportunity to salvage a project that might otherwise be in jeopardy.

carpenter's wood filler: Slightly different in consistency from epoxy putty, carpenter's wood filler proves handy for fixing up small carving boo-boos, such as a stray V-tooled trench, or for blending the seam between two laminated pieces of wood.

fine-grit sandpaper: Fine-grit sandpaper is great for removing what I call stray wood "hairies," which are tiny, ragged wood fibers that loosen up during the carving process.

stylus: Very versatile and can be used to trace patterns and to apply tiny dots of paint, glue, and other liquids. If you use a stylus to trace around patterns when transferring them to a block of wood, it keeps the patterns nice so they can be reused. Styluses come in a variety of point widths, making them handy for many uses. They are often found in craft stores.

baling wire: Bailing wire comes in a variety of diameters and is great for wire doweling small parts together.

cyanoacrylate glue: Quickly bonds wood, which can facilitate all kinds of repairs.

wood glue: If you don't have quick-grip glue, traditional wood glue will suffice. I also use wood glue when laminating several large boards together. For the most part, I find the quick-grip glue much more efficient than wood glue and use it almost exclusively.

old toothbrush: There is nothing like a soft old toothbrush for brushing away wood hairies and tiny wood chips from carvings. I keep several of them around because they do such a great job.

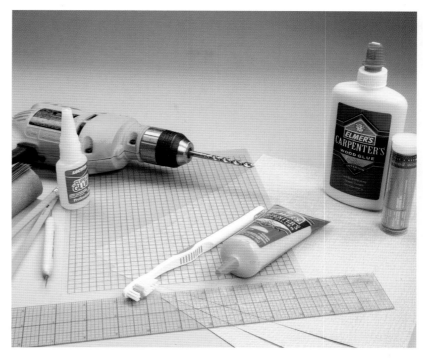

quilter's template plastic grid: I carried over this tool from my quilting projects because it worked so much better than using paper patterns. On occasion, you may want to use a template to make more than one of the same carving. For example, you may want to carve a project for several different people for Christmas or to sell at craft fairs. If you transfer the pattern onto the gridded plastic, rather than paper or card stock, it lasts forever, and you can make as many of the exact same thing as you wish. When cut into a 1" wide x 6 " long strip, gridded template plastic can also be a flexible ruler. It will wrap around carvings that would otherwise be difficult to measure. I keep several of these around and have given them to all of my carving friends.

manual or power drill: I also use a manual drill that holds small diameter bits, such as $\frac{1}{16}$" and $\frac{1}{32}$" drill bits. I use the manual drill for wire doweling and attaching small parts. I use the power drill for wood dowling.

Additional supplies. Many common household items can be very useful in your carving pursuits.

basic techniques

Once you have made a space for carving and gathered up your tools, it's time to learn some basic techniques. In this part, we'll go over the methods for using patterns, making cuts, and painting and finishing.

Choosing the correct method of transfer for your patterns is another essential part of a successful carving experience. By using some of the different methods demonstrated here, you'll learn what methods work best for different types of projects and discover which ones work best for you.

We'll then move on to making the different types of cuts with knives and gouges and also practice stropping the different tools to keep a sharp edge for carving.

Finally, we'll look at the variety of finishing techniques you can use to color and to protect your finished work. I've included a small section on doweling to help you assemble projects with multiple pieces.

transferring patterns

For beginners, being able to choose and use the right pattern is important for a successful carving experience. Many carving books include patterns for projects. There are also pattern packets available. The packets usually include a pattern for a band sawn shape and photos of the four different sides of the project. And that's it!

In my experience, pattern packets are of little use to a person with minimal carving experience because there are no directions for how to get from the band sawn shape to the finished product. That is why I have included step-by-step photos. They take you through the entire process, not merely provide you with the pattern. I start with easy patterns so, if you follow the directions, your finished project should look reasonably like mine. A pattern is a great starting place, and I encourage you to use my patterns as a foundation. Then, eventually, when you are ready, use your own creativity to develop a style of your own.

There are many different pattern transfer methods, and you will learn some of them in the subsequent pages. The degree of accuracy needed dictates whether tracing is adequate or if a more precise method needs to be employed. If you want cutouts that are virtually identical, then a template is required. If you want a sign with a nice, square, even border, using the pattern as a guide works best. Following are my preferred methods for transferring patterns.

adding registration lines

Though this technique is not used by itself, adding registration lines is very useful in conjunction with other methods of pattern transfer. It allows you to find the center point on the top and the bottom of a block of wood. Because a frequent challenge with beginning carvers is the ability to keep the carving centered, adding registration marks and then referring to them during the carving process aids in keeping the carving centered on the block of wood. To add registration lines, connect opposite corners on the top and the bottom of each block of wood to create an *X*. The middle of that *X* marks the center point of the wood. The method can be used on all blocks of wood that will be used for carving.

Registration lines. An *X* drawn from corner to corner on the top and the bottom of the block will help you find the center of the wood.

Photocopy or tissue paper transfer. Sandwich a piece of graphite paper between a photocopy or a tissue paper copy of the pattern and the wood to transfer patterns.

tissue paper transfer

The easiest way to use most patterns in this book is to photocopy them. However, if you do not have access to a photocopy machine, you can trace the patterns onto tissue paper by placing a piece of tissue paper over the pattern and tracing. Then, sandwich a piece of graphite paper, carbon side down, between the pattern and the wood, and trace over the lines with a stylus. Tissue paper transfer can be used on all projects carved from blocks of wood.

Gridded plastic templates. Trace the pattern onto a piece of gridded plastic, and then cut it out for a long-lasting, flexible template.

Tracing with a plastic template. Trace around the plastic template to transfer the pattern to the wood.

templates

Templates are used to create wooden cutouts. For example, the ornaments in the Halloween Cutouts project on page 38 are made with templates. The advantage of the template is you can use it multiple times and get the exact same outline or shape on the wood each time. If you wanted to sell several of the same project at a craft fair, you would use templates for consistency in your work. If you were to use a tissue paper transfer, you might get different but similar shapes each time.

patterns as guides

Any time you want to transfer a pattern that consists basically of straight lines, you can use the pattern to mark each line at the corner point of the wood and then connect the dots with a ruler. The method makes for a more precise pattern transfer. I use this technique on the *Beware Sign* on page 108. The border of squares will be much more precise if you look at the pattern, use it to measure the depth of the border, transfer the measurement to the wood, and use a ruler to make a nice, even, precise border line. Use the pattern again to make tiny slash marks for each square and again connect the slash marks using a ruler to end up with a crisp, accurate border instead of tracing the pattern and ending up with wiggly lines. Using the pattern as a guide is more accurate, but it takes more time to transfer a pattern this way.

freehand transfer

Some patterns can't be transferred with a ruler or graphite paper. In those cases, you'll need to transfer your pattern freehand. Take a good look at the finished example and use your best judgment to transfer the lines to your piece of wood. Odds are that if you're using freehand transfer, the pattern doesn't have to be exact.

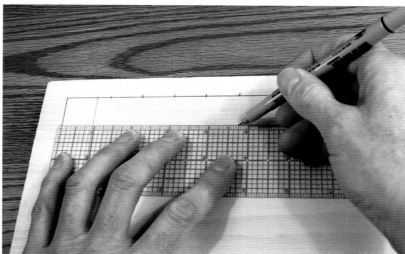

Using the pattern. Mark guidelines on the wood using the pattern as a guide, and connect these points with a ruler. Any remaining details can be transferred directly to the wood by sandwiching a piece of graphite paper between the paper and the wood.

making the basic cuts

You'll only have to deal with a few basic cuts to carve the featured projects. We'll go over each of them individually. Plan to refer to this section as you work your way through the step-by-step instructions for each project.

Before you practice the cuts, you'll need to determine the grain of the wood to ensure you carve *with* the grain rather than *against* it (see "Wood Grain" on page 14). Carving against the grain is difficult and will not produce good results. You also need to examine your wood for any chips, splits, or knots, and try to avoid those areas or incorporate them into the portions to be carved away.

the stop cut

Carving is really a pretty basic thing—scoring a line and then carving back to that line. The scored line is called your stop cut. A stop cut is a very simple but extremely useful technique.

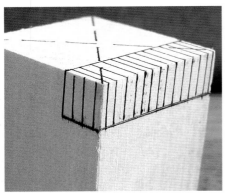

Shade the area. I draw a series of closely spaced parallel lines on the wood to shade the area where wood will be removed. I will refer throughout the book to these shaded areas. You may choose whether or not you wish to actually add the shading lines or just refer to the photos that show them. Here, I have shaded an area to be removed that is ¾" deep x 2" wide x ¾" long.

Make a stop cut. Pull the bench knife along the line you traced onto your wood. This is called scoring the wood, and it creates a stop cut. Score the line to about 1⁄16". Start at one edge and continue across the wood until you are about ¼" away from the other edge. Score back from the other edge to meet the line you just scored.

Carve back to the stop cut. With a #3 ⅝" or a #3 ⅞" gouge, carve back to the line you scored, removing thin slices of wood. This is called carving back to the stop cut. The stop cut we made will naturally interrupt the forward motion of the gouge. Note the slices of wood may not come off at this point. We'll take care of that in the next step. Never pull the slices off.

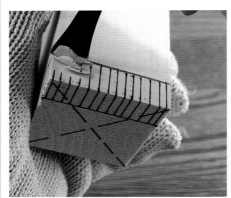

Deepen the stop cut. Retrace the original stop cut with a bench knife or use the gouge to deepen the stop cut and release these thin slices of wood.

Repeat the process. Continue removing thin slices of wood and deepening the stop cut.

The finished cut. When all of the wood in the shaded area has been removed, you should have a flat and level ledge.

the push cut

Sometimes you'll be carving a very fine detail. You'll want to use a controlled cut. To control your cut, place the knife in your hand and cut only as far as the thumbs of your opposite hand will push the knife without moving the rest of your hand.

the pull cut

The pull cut is the opposite of the push cut. To make the pull cut, you will be pulling the knife toward you in almost the same motion as you would use to pare an apple. The one major difference is the placement of the thumb of your carving hand. Always—and I do mean always—keep it out of the path of your knife. Carving knives are very sharp. Don't rely on a thumb guard to protect you from a cut.

cutting with a gouge

Gouges cut in two different ways: by hand and by mallet.

To make a cut with a gouge by hand, hold the gouge firmly in the palm of your hand and wrap your fingers around the handle. Bring the gouge toward you, with the palm of your hand facing up, as you cut. Again, keep the fingers and wrist of your other hand and your body out of the path of the gouge, and use a small range of motion. This is a controlled cut.

To make a cut with a gouge using a mallet, place the gouge against the wood and tap the mallet to move the gouge through the wood. The cut should only be done when the wood can be held securely to the workbench. Never use this technique when you are holding the wood in your lap.

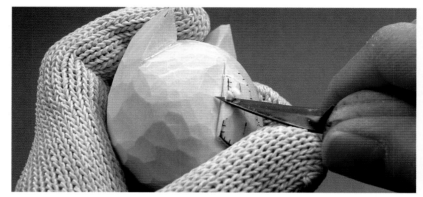

Push cut. Use the thumb of your opposite hand to push the blade of the knife away from you.

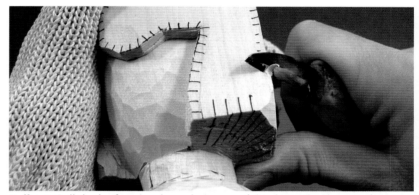

Pull cut. Pull the knife toward you, being careful to keep the thumb of your carving hand and your opposite hand out of the path of the knife.

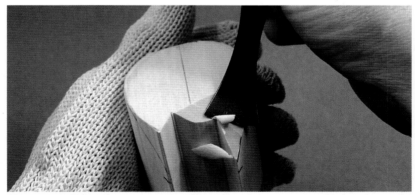

Gouge cut. Bring the gouge toward you, keeping your opposite hand out of the path of the gouge.

how to strop a knife

After you have carved for around 30 minutes, it's time to strop your tools. Stropping is easy to do and definitely worth the time you put into it. As I mentioned earlier, stropping is the process of honing the blade on a polishing surface to repolish the edges of the tool. A tool with highly polished edges will move through wood smoothly. You will learn to recognize that, when your tool feels as if it is beginning to drag through the wood, it is time to strop.

Stroping the blade 50 times on one side and 50 times on the other side will take only a few minutes, but it makes all the difference. Some carvers suggest you strop your tools 5 minutes for every 30 minutes of carving. My carving is always much more enjoyable if I just take that 5-minute preparation to get my tools back up to speed.

Remember, you can choose to strop with or without honing compound. If you do use honing compound, the type you choose—solid bars, cream, or others—is entirely up to you. Any type will help speed up the process.

what's a bevel?

The bevel of a knife simply refers to the angles on the sharpened edge. When you strop, be sure the bevel, not the side, of the knife is placed firmly against the leather.

The edge created by the two bevels makes a knife sharp. Keeping the bevels highly polished will ensure your knife is razor sharp.

1. Hold the strop in your left hand. Place the blade of the knife on the strop near the handle with the beveled edge of the knife toward you.

2. Push the knife along the leather to the far end of the strop with firm pressure. Make sure the bevel of the knife is in contact with the leather as you push. When you reach the end, lift the knife and return it to the leather near the handle. Repeat the step 50 times.

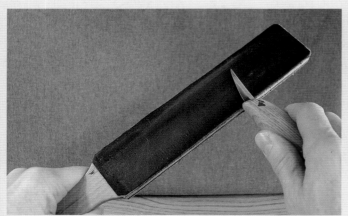

3. Now hold the knife at the far end of the strop with the beveled edge of the knife away from you.

4. Pull the knife along the length of the strop, from the far end toward the handle, using firm pressure. Make sure the bevel is in contact with the leather as you pull. When you reach the handle, lift the knife and return it to the far end of the strop. Repeat the step 50 times.

how to strop a gouge

Stropping a gouge is similar to stropping a knife, but all edges of the curved surface of the gouge must be polished. You can choose to strop with or without honing compound. I've used it for this demonstration. My honing compound is a microfine green chromium oxide compound. It comes in a bar, and I rub it over the strop before I begin the stropping process. If you choose a slip strop, when you hone your tools, use the honing compound that comes with the strop.

If you use a slip strop and all surfaces of the bevel contact the channel of the strop, you do not need to rotate the gouge or strop the gouge in sections. The inside surface of the gouge also must be stropped. The slip strop has a variety of shaped profiles to fit the inside surfaces of a variety of gouges.

curved bevel

A gouge has one less bevel than a knife, but it can be more challenging to strop because you must hone all sections of the curved bevel. As with stropping a knife, the bevel of a gouge, not its sides, need to be in contact with the leather.

The gouge has only one beveled edge, but the curve of that bevel can make it more challenging to strop.

Using a Flat Strop

1. If you are using a flat strop, you need to strop the gouge in sections. Hold the gouge at the far end of the strop with the left bevel of the gouge on the strop. Pull the gouge toward you, making sure the left side of the bevel is in contact with the leather. Repeat 50 times.

2. Rotate the gouge slightly so the center part of the bevel is in contact with the strop leather. Strop 50 times, pulling the gouge toward you.

3. Finally, rotate the gouge so the right edge of the bevel is in contact with the strop leather. Strop 50 times, pulling the gouge toward you. The larger-sweep gouges will require more rotations to address all sections of the gouge.

Using a Slip Strop

1. Fit the gouge, rounded side down, into the far edge of the appropriate channel. Pull the gouge down the length of the strop with firm pressure. When you reach the end of the strop, lift the gouge and return it to the far end of the strop. Repeat 50 times.

2. Find the surface most like the inside surface of the gouge you wish to strop. Place the gouge at the far side of the strop, inside surface on the curved strop surface. Pull the gouge down the length of the strop with firm pressure. When you reach the end, lift the gouge and return it to the far end of the strop. Repeat 50 times.

painting and finishing techniques

After you have completed your carving project, you must decide how to finish it. Among your finishing choices are painting, staining, antiquing, and applying oil and paste wax. You may choose any one of these or a combination to suit your purposes. In choosing, you should consider your personal taste, the type of carving, what it will be used for, the kind of wood, if it will be handled frequently, and whether it will be exposed to the elements.

Finishing products produce beautiful results but must be used with care. Before we talk about specific finishes, read "Safety Tips" below.

Safety Tips

- Remember to always follow the manufacturer's safety precautions when applying any finish.

- Wear latex gloves because finishes are messy and may contain resins and other elements that could be harmful if absorbed into your body.

- Work in a well-ventilated area. Many finishes are combustible and have harmful vapors.

- If you use cloth rags to apply oil, always lay them out flat and allow them to dry before disposing of them. Oil products produce heat as they dry and, if not properly used, can spontaneously combust. Wadding up an oily cloth and throwing it in a trash can is creating the potential for a fire.

A painted finish. Paint adds color and provides a small amount of protection for your carving. Basswood projects are often painted because of their mild grain patterns. A painted project is typically finished with varnish or paste wax.

painting

Any wood can be painted with acrylic, oil, or latex paint. As I mentioned earlier, basswood is one of the most popular woods for carving, but it does not have the beautiful wood grain of other woods. Because the wood is so plain, items carved out of basswood are typically painted.

I believe acrylic paint is the most convenient because it cleans up very easily. Your color choices may be subtle or bold, dramatic or fun—whatever emotion you wish to express. Avoid using full-strength paint directly out of the bottle because it is too thick, does not flow, and fills in fine details you probably don't want to have filled in. Instead, thin the paint with water. Remember to use good quality brushes for your carvings.

If you decide to paint your carving, it then needs to be finished with varnish or paste wax. If the carving will be exposed to the elements (outside), finish with a spar varnish.

To paint your carving:

Step 1: Apply a wash that is one part water and one part acrylic paint. Using a wash for the first coat allows you to easily get paint into all of the cracks and crevices, and allows the paint to soak into the wood a little bit. Allow the first coat to dry 15 minutes before applying the second coat. Flat brushes in sizes 2 to 8 are good for blocking in base colors.

Step 2: Follow up with a second coat of paint thinned with water only slightly, to the consistency of cream. The water allows the paint to flow more easily, but the mixture still provides adequate color coverage.

Step 3: Use a #0 or #1 liner brush to add details.

staining

There may be occasions when you would like your carving to take on the appearance of another wood. To achieve that effect, you would use a wood stain. Normally, stains are applied to woods that have a visible grain pattern, but they may be used on any wood. Stains are thinner in consistency than paint and are often applied with a cloth or a disposable foam brush in the same manner as paint. Stain can be messy and will stay on your brush, so avoid using good paintbrushes for staining. Stains come in a variety of finishes—oak, maple, walnut, cherry, and pine, for example.

To stain your carving:

Step 1: Apply the stain per the manufacturer's directions. Use a disposable foam brush to apply the first coat of stain. Typically, the wood is covered with an even, thin coat of stain. Maintain an even color as you are applying the stain.

Step 2: A second coat may be required depending on the richness of color you desire. Allow each coat to dry thoroughly before adding the next. A stained project will typically be finished with varnish or paste wax.

A varnished finish.
Water-based varnish may foam as it is applied. Varnish protects painted surfaces and adds a rich luster to projects.

varnishing

There are many types of varnish. For the projects in this book, a water-based varnish is a good choice because it is easy to apply. Varnishing is another method of finishing that does not block out the wood grain, but it works best over paint. It basically involves applying thin coats of varnish with a paintbrush. Typically, the more thin coats you apply, the nicer the finish. If you just put on one thick coat, you may get a lot of air bubbles, so multiple thin coats work best.

Cleanup with water-based varnish is very easy and requires only soap and water. Carvings finished with water-based varnish would be for interior use only. If your carving will be exposed to the elements, you need to finish it with a spar varnish product. Apply the product according to the manufacturer's directions.

To varnish your carving:

Step 1: Using a ¾" wash brush, apply one thin coat of varnish (one part water-based varnish and one part water) to the project after the paint is dry. Varnish may foam as you apply it.

Step 2: After a minute or two, brush over the varnished area to smooth out any bubbles. Wait 15 minutes.

Step 3: Then, apply a second thin coat. Again brush away any remaining bubbles after a minute or two. Allow the piece to dry overnight.

antiquing

If you like the look that age brings to a carving, you may want to consider antiquing. It is easy to do and nicely highlights the details of your carving. The antiquing process is done over a painted and varnished piece. Quite different and not necessarily desirable results will be experienced if the painted piece is not varnished before the antiquing is applied. Once you have painted and varnished a piece, you can make an antiquing mixture out of any color of paint that will complement your carving by adding that color paint to antiquing medium/retarder. Typically, you would use a brown shade of paint. My favorite is a mixture of one part burnt sienna, one part raw sienna, and two parts antiquing retarder. For more subtle antiquing, use one part dark flesh and one part antiquing retarder.

Since antiquing involves wiping off the bulk of the antiquing mixture, try not to leave it on any longer than you have to. On larger pieces, I will antique one section at a time. The antiquing mixture allows you several minutes of working time, but I don't like to risk having it dry before I am able to remove as much of the mixture as I want. I used this technique on the *Beware Sign* found on page 108 in this book.

To antique your carving:

Step 1: Create an antiquing mixture to suit your project.

Step 2: When the antiquing mixture is ready, use an old, worn-out brush to completely cover the carving (or sections of a large carving) with the antiquing mixture. Don't be timid about mashing your old brush into the cracks and crevices and using it to really scrub the antiquing mixture on the carving. Completely covering the carving with antiquing mixture is the key to the antiquing process.

Step 3: With a soft cloth (or a cotton swab in small areas), wipe off the antiquing mixture until the piece has the look you want. Allow the piece to dry thoroughly.

An antiqued finish.
Antiquing is easy to do, and it emphasizes the details of your carving.

oil

Oil finishes have been used for centuries to preserve wood and to bring out its natural beauty. Unlike finishes that remain on the surface, oil penetrates the wood and is absorbed into the fibers where it hardens and forms a strong finish. Oil finishes are easy to apply and offer added protection to the wood. Linseed oil and tung oil cure and work well as finishes. If you use linseed oil, be sure to use boiled linseed oil because it has an added drying agent that helps the finish dry faster. Without this additive, the finish could take a week or more to dry. Boiled linseed oil often takes a week or less. Tung oil does not require a drying agent and cures in several days.

To create an oil finish for your carving:

Step 1: Apply oil to the carving with an old paintbrush or a soft cloth. Allow the carving to soak up the oil for about an hour.

Step 2: Then, using a soft cloth, wipe off any remaining oil. Allow the carving to dry for 12 hours.

Step 3: Apply a second coat of oil. After 15 minutes, wipe off any remaining oil. Allow the oil to cure for several days. Once the oil has cured, the carving can be left as it is or you can apply a coat of paste wax to finish it.

paste wax

To add a rich luster to your carving, to enhance its beauty, and to give it a nice, hard finish, you might want to apply a paste wax. Paste waxes were very popular when everyone had wood floors, but now you do not hear about them much. Minwax makes a very nice paste wax that works well on woodcarvings. Paste wax can be used as a final finish on any carving. For example, you can use it alone, over stain, or over a painted surface.

To add a paste wax finish to your carving:

Step 1: Place some paste wax in a double layer of cheesecloth and rub it over the carving. Use this method to apply a thin, even coat of paste wax to the entire carving. Allow the wax to dry 10 to 15 minutes.

Step 2: Then, polish the carving with a soft, clean cloth. Use some elbow grease to get a highly polished shine.

Combining Finishes

Different combinations of finishes can achieve different effects. Since, for example, acrylic paint dries very flat, some further finish is needed. Here are the most common ways, and the best orders, to use finishes on a project.

Finishing Possibilities for Painted Projects	Finishing Possibilities for Unpainted Projects
Paint, then varnish	Oil
Paint, then varnish, then antique	Oil, then paste wax
Paint, then varnish, then antique, then paste wax	Stain (oil based), then oil, then paste wax

doweling

Some carvings consist of auxiliary pieces of wood adhered to the main piece of wood. Doweling is a way to ensure the connections will be strong.

For this book, we'll use two different doweling techniques. One uses a wooden dowel to connect two parts of a carving; the other uses a wire to connect the pieces. Both methods use glue to make sure the connection stays tight.

Sometimes doweling is done after a carving has been painted and finished. It is much easier to paint and finish the boots separately and then attach them than it is to apply paint or finish to a fully assembled piece. The exception to this would be when arms or other integral parts of the carving are added. It is necessary to add them and blend them into the main carving before you paint or finish.

wood doweling

Wood doweling uses lengths of ¼" dowel rods to connect the pieces of the carving. The process is simple, but you have to do some preliminary planning to get it right. Take the time to dry fit the pieces together and trace the outlines as explained below. Otherwise, you may end up with holes on the outside of your carving instead of at the joint where they belong. This technique is used to join the legs to the body in the Witch project on page 80.

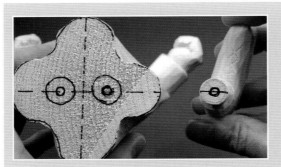

Wood Doweling

Trace. Dry fit the pieces you wish to join together. Transfer the outline of the bottom piece to the top piece. Make sure the piece is balanced. You don't want it tipping over after the legs are added. Draw lines to connect opposite corners or edges to find the center point of each piece. Draw these lines on the bottom of the top piece and on the top of the bottom piece. Plan carefully!

Drill. With a hand drill and a ¼" drill bit, drill a ½"-deep hole at the center point of each piece.

Glue. Glue a 1" length of ¼" dowel in one of the pieces using Beacon "Quick Grip" All-Purpose Permanent Adhesive. Again, dry fit doweled piece into receiving piece to make sure everything fits. Add more Quick Grip to the remaining exposed dowel and the wood surrounding the dowel. Insert into corresponding hole. Allow them to dry.

wire doweling

When attaching small pieces, you can substitute wire for a wooden dowel. Be sure to dry fit all of the pieces before you glue. This technique is used to attach the arm to the body in the Witch project on page 80.

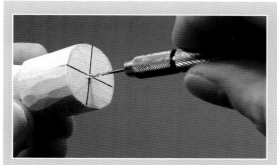

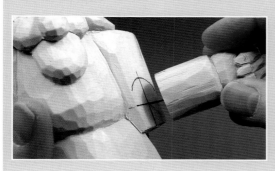

Wire Doweling

Drill. Using a stylus or a manual hand drill and a ¹⁄₁₆" drill bit, make a hole in the center of the witch's lower arm. Then, make a corresponding hole in the center of the witch's upper arm.

Glue. With cyanoacrylate glue, adhere a ½" length of baling wire into the hole in the lower arm. Dry fit the arm with the wire into the corresponding hole in the upper arm. Apply a narrow ring of Quick Grip around the wood surrounding the wire. Add a drop of cyanoacrylate glue to the remaining end of the wire, and then insert the wire into the hole in the upper arm, as shown. Allow to dry for 15 minutes.

projects

All that remains is to put your carving skills to good use to create the projects presented here. I'll take you step-by-step through some Halloween ornaments, a mummy, a cat in pumpkins, two trick-or-treaters, and a witch. Then, once you've made your way through those step-by-step projects, I've included two additional projects for you to try—the Beware Sign and the Halloween Candy Bowl. These two projects are built on the carving techniques you will already have learned by completing the rest of the Halloween carvings in the book. Give them a try, and don't be afraid to experiment with ideas of your own.

project 1 halloween cutouts

Start your Halloween carving fun by trying these easy-to-make items. Each object is carved from a piece of ⅜" stock. Add carved details or just a coat of paint, and then mix them and match them to create unique projects. I decorated my porch with a candy corn garland made from cutouts, and I hung Halloween ornaments around the house.

tools and supplies

carving

- ⅜"-thick stock for ornaments
- 1¼" x ¾" x ⅜" basswood blocks for candy corn
- Gridded plastic
- Black fine-line marker
- Pencil
- Carving knife
- Detail knife
- #3 ⅞" gouge
- #9 5 mm gouge
- 1 mm V-tool
- Drill with ⁵⁄₆₄" bit

painting and finishing

- Acrylic paint, such as Delta Ceramcoat, in the following colors:
    Apple green
    Black
    Charcoal
    Dark flesh
    Hunter green
    Lichen grey
    Light ivory
    Opaque yellow
    Pumpkin
    Quaker grey
    Tangerine

- Flat brushes in sizes 2 to 8 for blocking color
- #0 or #1 liner brushes for detail painting
- Stiff-bristle round brush

varnishing

- Water-based satin-finish varnish, mixed one part water to one part varnish (see page 31 for varnishing directions)
- ¾" wash brush or small flat brush for smaller parts

antiquing

- Antiquing medium/retarder, such as Jo Sonja's (see page 32 for antiquing directions)
- Acrylic paint, such as Delta Ceramcoat, in the following colors:
    Burnt sienna
    Raw sienna
- Old flat brush
- Soft cloth or old T-shirt
- Cotton swabs

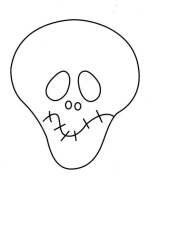

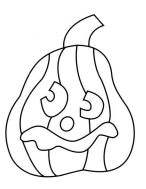

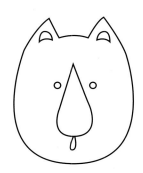

for candy
corn garland

1 Begin with several small blocks 1¼" x ¾" x ⅜" basswood. Candy corn blocks are shown here.

2 Make gridded plastic templates from the patterns. Trace the patterns onto ⅜"-stock.

3 In order to string the candy corn garland later, drill a hole completely through the wood block on the ⅜" side, ¼" from the top, with a ⁵⁄₆₄" bit.

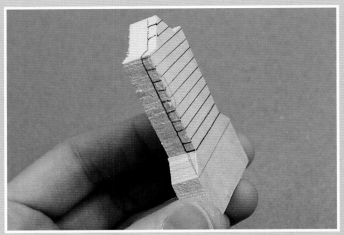

4 With a pencil, mark any areas of excess wood to be removed, such as the front of the tombstone shown here.

5 Use a #3 ⅞" gouge to remove the excess wood.

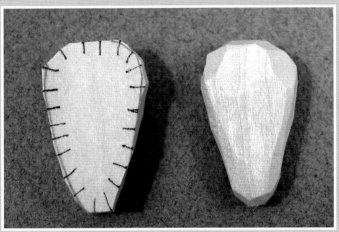

6 Round the edges of the cutouts with a carving or detail knife, as shown here.

7 Use a detail knife to outline and remove wood from the larger features, like the eyes, nose, and mouth of the pumpkin shown here.

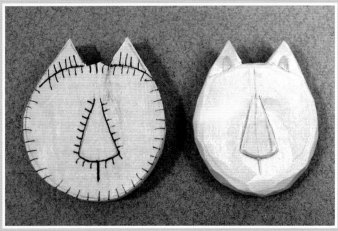

8 Use a #9 5 mm gouge to carve indentations, like the cat's ears shown here. (A detail knife was used to score the lines and remove a thin layer of wood around the nose and ears.)

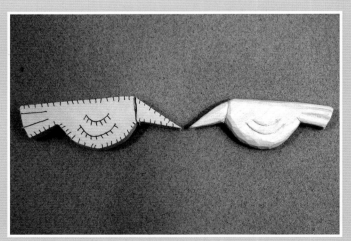

9 Add any details, such as the wings and tail feathers shown here, with a 1 mm V-tool. Because I like to see the carved facets on the wood, I do not sand before finishing. The carved cutouts are now ready to be painted and assembled into the project of your choice.

painting and finishing

Paint the cutouts according to the color chart or using your own imagination. You can use the cutouts in a variety of ways. I've included two suggestions for you on pages 42–43.

General instructions

1. Base coat each piece with two coats of each color paint (see page 30). Allow the carving to dry.
2. Add any painted details.
3. When the paint is completely dry, apply two coats of a water-based varnish (see page 31).
4. Scrub the antiquing mixture into the cracks and crevices with an old brush (see page 32).
5. Wipe away any excess antiquing mixture with a soft cloth. Use a cotton swab to remove the antiquing mixture from any tight spaces.
6. Allow each piece to dry thoroughly.

COLOR CHART

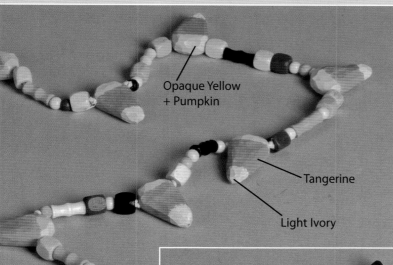

Opaque Yellow + Pumpkin

Tangerine

Light Ivory

Candy corn and ornaments are antiqued with one part burnt sienna, one part raw sienna, and two parts antiquing medium.

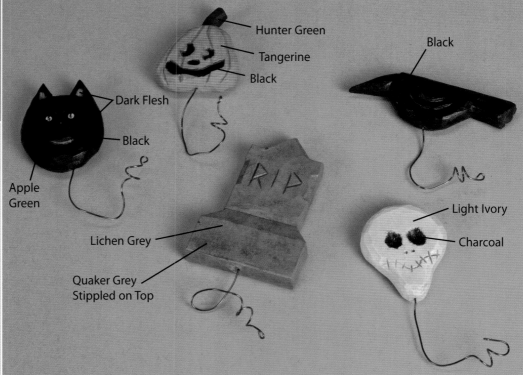

Hunter Green

Tangerine

Black

Black

Dark Flesh

Black

Apple Green

Light Ivory

Charcoal

Lichen Grey

Quaker Grey Stippled on Top

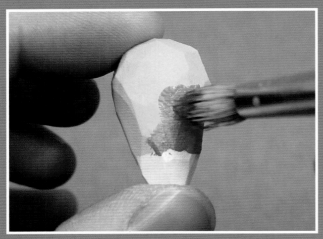

1 Base coat the whole candy corn cutout using two coats of light ivory. Then, paint two coats of yellow (opaque yellow mixed with a tiny amount of pumpkin) on the remainder of the candy corn, leaving the white tip.

2 Using a stiff bristle round brush, add one coat of tangerine by bouncing the brush up and down in a stipple technique to create an uneven band of orange, as shown.

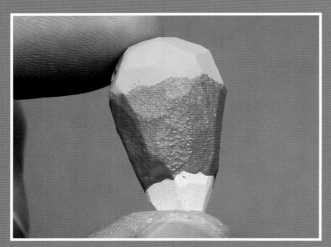

3 Varnish and antique the cutouts, and allow them to dry thoroughly.

Candy Corn Garland

This simple candy corn garland is a great project for beginners of all ages. The pieces are easy to carve, and assembling the garland requires no sewing needles. The finished garland is perfect to be hung almost anywhere.

tools and supplies

- Carved candy corn cutouts (pattern on page 39)
- Acrylic paint, such as Delta Ceramcoat, in the following colors:
    Light ivory
    Opaque yellow
    Pumpkin
    Tangerine
- Flat brush
- Stiff-bristle round brush
- Water-based varnish, mixed one part water to one part varnish (see page 31)
- Antiquing retarder, such as Jo Sonja's, mixed two parts antiquing medium to one part burnt sienna and one part raw sienna (see page 32 for application instructions)
- Assorted wooden beads purchased from a craft store
- 54" of 20 lb. hemp cord
- Hand drill and ⁵⁄₆₄" drill bit

4 String the finished candy corn and a variety of wooden beads onto a 54" length of 20 lb. hemp cord. The cord is stiff enough that no needle is required to string the beads.

Halloween Ornaments

Creating ornaments is another fun and simple way to use the Halloween cutouts. You can use your imagination to paint them any color you like, and adding wire is quick and easy. Hang them on a tree or anywhere you wish.

tools and supplies

- Assorted carved Halloween cutouts (patterns on page 39)
- Acrylic paint, such as Delta Ceramcoat, in the following colors:
    - Apple green
    - Black
    - Charcoal
    - Dark flesh
    - Hunter green
    - Lichen grey
    - Light ivory
    - Quaker grey
    - Tangerine
- Flat brushes in sizes 2 to 8 for blocking color
- #0 or #1 liner brushes for detail painting
- Water-based satin-finish varnish , mixed one part water to one part varnish (see page 31 for application instructions)
- Antiquing retarder, such as Jo Sonja's, mixed two parts antiquing medium to one part burnt sienna and one part raw sienna (see page 32 for application instructions)
- Hand drill and ¹⁄₁₆" drill bit
- 4" length of 22-gauge brown coated wire for each hanger
- Cyanoacrylate glue

1. Paint the carved ornaments using the colors suggested.
2. Varnish and antique each ornament, and allow them to dry thoroughly.
3. Use a hand drill and a ¹⁄₁₆" drill bit to drill a ¼" hole near the top of each Halloween ornament.
4. Apply a dot of cyanoacrylate glue to the end of a 4" length of 22-gauge brown coated wire. Insert the end of the wire into the ornament. Allow the glue to dry.

project 2 mummy

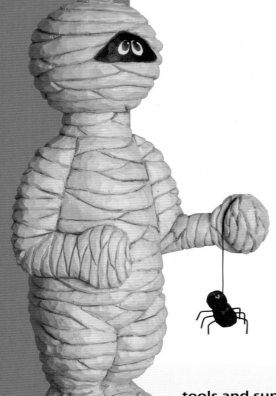

Here's a fun figure to decorate a tabletop or any surface you like. When we carve this figure, we'll be using many of the basic cuts, and we'll practice carving details to create the mummy's many layers of bandages.

tools and supplies

carving
- 1⅛" x 1⅛" x 1¾" basswood block for left arm
- 2½" x 2½" x 8" basswood block for body
- ⅜" x ⅜" x ⅞" basswood block for spider
- Bench knife
- Detail knife
- #3 ⅞" gouge
- Band saw
- Hand drill and ¹⁄₁₆" drill bit
- Baling wire to dowel arm to body
- Six ½" lengths of 22-gauge black coated wire for spider legs
- One 2" length of black elastic sewing thread
- Cyanoacrylate glue

painting
- Acrylic paint, such as Delta Ceramcoat, in the following colors:
    Autumn brown
    Black
    Dark brown
    Light ivory
    Old parchment
- Flat brushes in sizes 2 to 8 for blocking color
- #0 or #1 liner brushes for detail painting

varnishing
- Satin-finish water-based varnish (see page 31 for application instructions), mixed one part water to one part varnish
- ¾" wash brush or small flat brush for smaller parts

antiquing
- Antiquing medium/retarder, such as Jo Sonja's (see page 32 for antiquing directions)
- Acrylic paint, such as Delta Ceramcoat, in the following colors:
    Burnt sienna
    Raw sienna
- Old flat brush
- Soft cloth or old T-shirt
- Cotton swabs

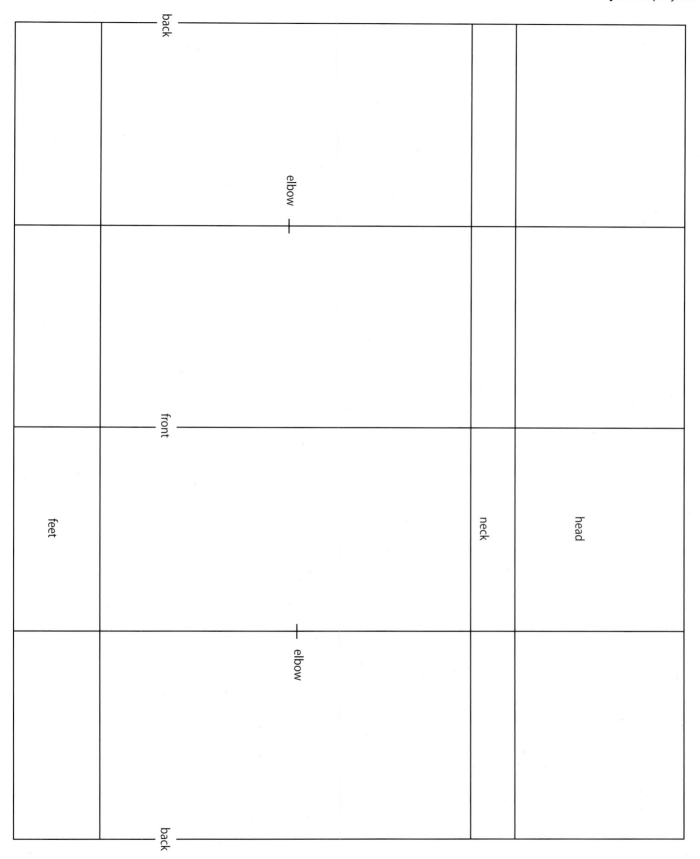

back

elbow

front

feet

neck

head

elbow

back

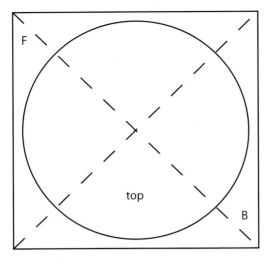

top

F

B

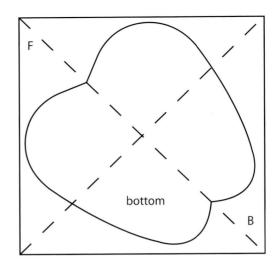

bottom

F

B

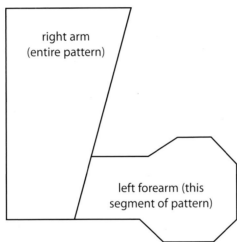

right arm
(entire pattern)

left forearm (this
segment of pattern)

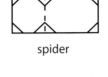

spider

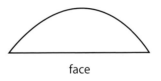

face

© Cyndi Joslyn

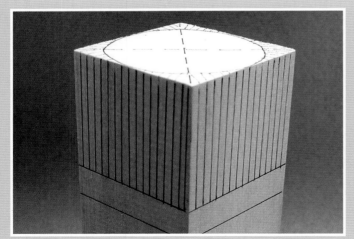

1 Transfer the body pattern to the block of wood sized for the body. I like to shade the wood to indicate areas that should be removed.

2 Score the line beneath the shaded area with a bench knife, and use a #3 ⅞" gouge to form an evenly rounded cylinder for the mummy's head.

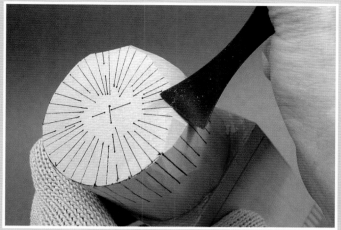

3 Shade the wood to be removed. Use either the #3 ⅞" gouge or the bench knife to round the top of the mummy's head.

4 Continue rounding with the gouge or the bench knife until the mummy's head is evenly rounded. This is how your project should look at this point.

5 Score the bottom of the mummy's head with the bench knife.

6 Continue to remove wood in thin layers with the #3 ⅞" gouge to further define the mummy's head.

7 The mummy's head at the top of the neck will be 1" in from the corners and ½" in from the sides.

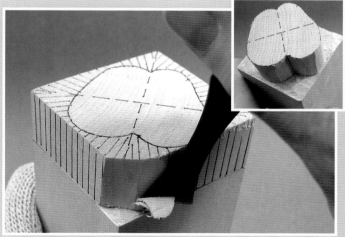

8 Wood in the shaded area will be removed to create the mummy's feet. Score the line above the shaded area, and use the #3 ⅞" gouge to remove the wood.

halloween woodcarving 47

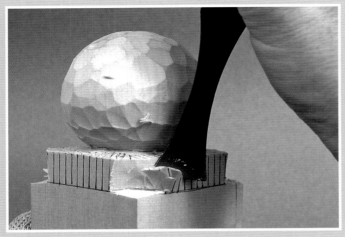

9 Use the #3 ⅞" gouge to remove the wood in the shaded area to create the mummy's neck.

10 A detail knife works well for removing wood where the neck recedes under the head. The bottom of the neck will be 1⅛" in from the corners and ⅝" in from the sides.

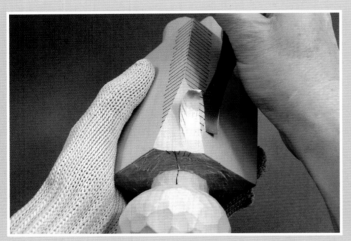

11 Remove the wood in the shaded area, and round it using the #3 ⅞" gouge.

12 Draw the arm patterns on the front and back of the mummy, as shown.

13 Using the bench knife, score around the arms and remove the wood in the shaded areas to define the arms.

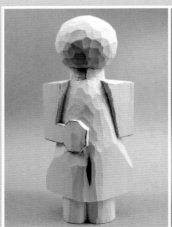

14 Continue blocking in the arms. The progress to this point shows the mummy's head and neck defined and the feet and arms blocked in.

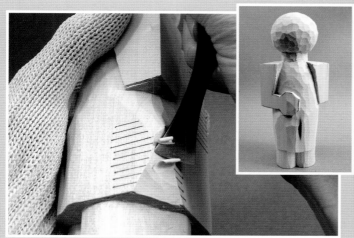

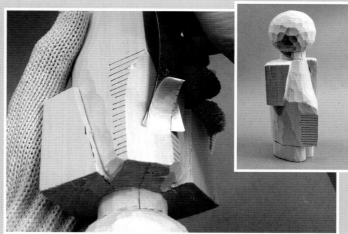

15 Remove the wood in the shaded area on both sides of the mummy to further define the legs. The #3 ⅞" gouge works well for this step.

16 Remove the wood in the shaded area to define the mummy's back. Use the #3 ⅞" gouge and a scooping motion to remove the wood. Round the wood in the shaded area to begin to define the legs.

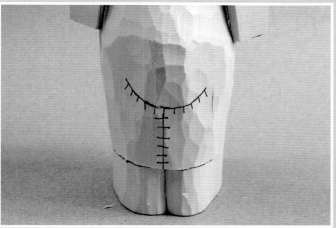

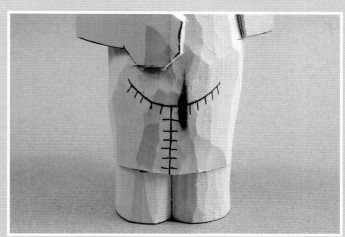

17 Extend the centerline up from the base of the feet 2¼" on the back. Draw a curved line to define the mummy's tush, as shown. This curved line is about 1½" wide.

18 Extend the centerline up from the base of the feet 2⅜" on the front. Draw a curved line to define the mummy's lower belly. This line is about 1½" wide.

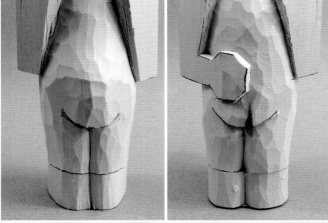

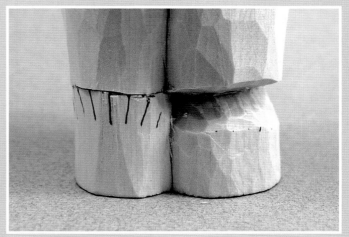

19 Use the bench knife or the detail knife to score these lines and remove wood, as shown, to define the legs on the front and the back.

20 With the bench knife, score around the top of the feet and remove the wood in the shaded area to shape the feet.

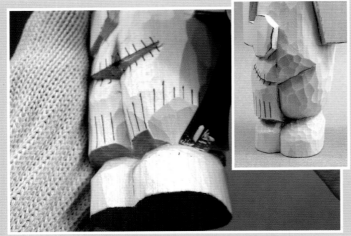

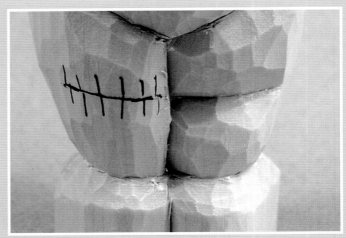

21 Remove the wood in the shaded area with the bench knife to further define the legs on the front and back and to round the belly and tush.

22 On the back of the mummy, draw a line to define the back of the knees. This line is about 1" wide and up 1½" from the bottom edge of the feet.

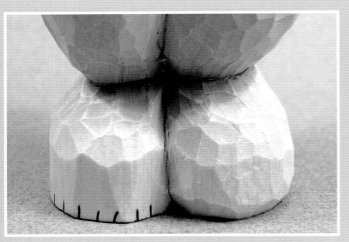

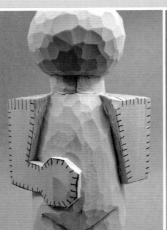

23 Use the bench knife or the detail knife to round the edges of the feet.

24 Mark the wood to be removed from the sharp corners of the mummy's arms and hands.

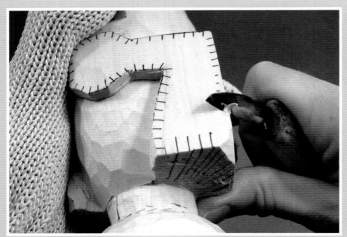

25 Round the edges of the arms, front and back, using the bench knife.

26 Continue rounding the arms until they are well defined. The progress to this point illustrates clearly defined legs, belly, and tush. The mummy's arms and feet have also been defined.

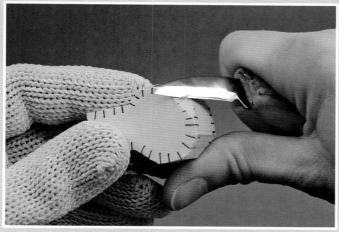

27 Band saw the pattern for the left forearm from 1" stock. With the bench knife, round the wood in the shaded area to shape the forearm.

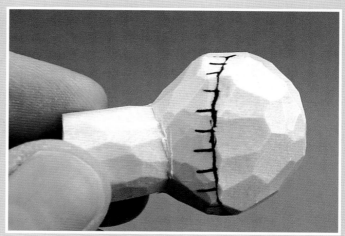

28 Draw the line for the hand, as shown.

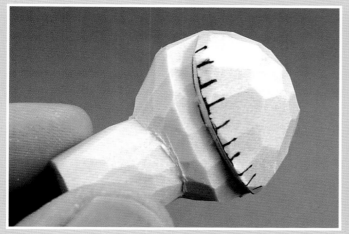

29 Remove a small amount of wood in the shaded area below the line to define the hand.

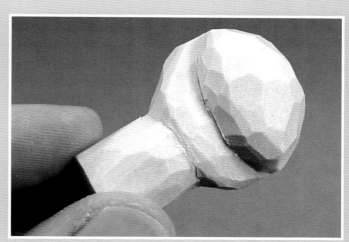

30 Round the edges of the hand.

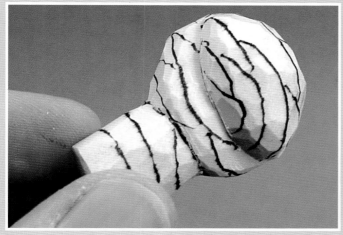

31 Draw a random circular pattern on the forearm to create the rags that wrap the mummy.

32 Score the lines and remove a small amount of wood under each line using the detail knife.

33 Use the bench knife to carve a deep line across the face of one side of the ball to show where the fingers overlap the palm of the hand.

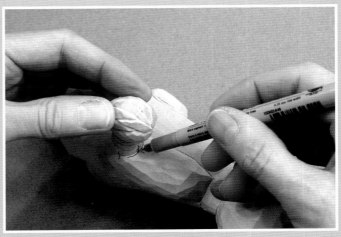

34 Line up the left forearm to the desired position near the left elbow and trace this position onto the body.

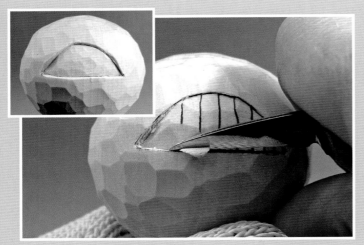

35 Transfer the face pattern. Score the outline and remove a small amount of wood with the detail knife, as shown.

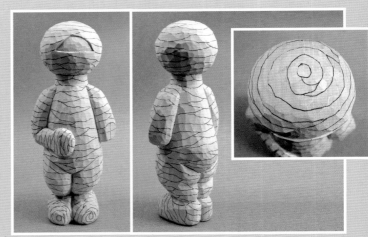

36 Draw a random circular pattern on the mummy to simulate the rags that wrap the body.

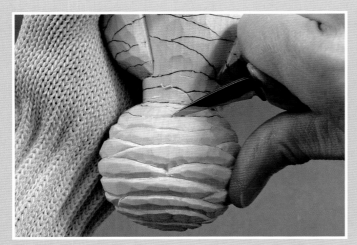

37 Score all the lines and remove a small amount of wood under each line using the detail knife.

38 Glue the arm in place using the wire doweling technique (see page 38).

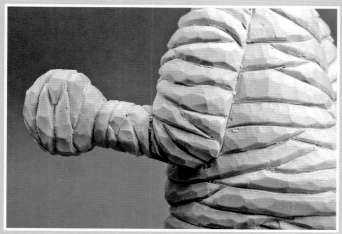

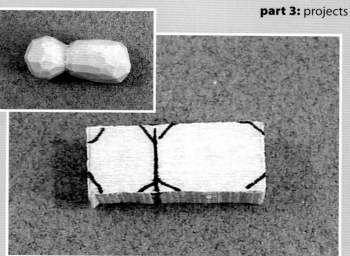

39 With the bench knife, blend the arm sections together. Draw a circular pattern to connect the sections.

40 Transfer the spider pattern to the block, and round the segments with the detail knife.

41 The mummy and the spider are now ready for painting.

Painting and finishing

Paint the mummy and the spider using the colors listed in the supplies list and in the color chart. Varnish and antique the mummy and spider; then, follow the step-by-step instructions to assemble the carving.

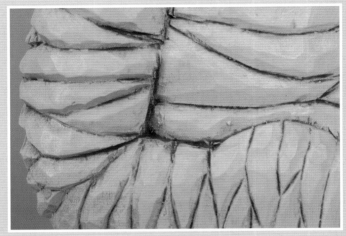

1 Before assembling, varnish and antique the mummy and spider.

2 Using a hand drill and a ¹⁄₁₆" drill bit, drill a hole at the center point where the spider head and body connect, as shown. Also drill three holes in each side of the spider at the points highlighted by the white dots.

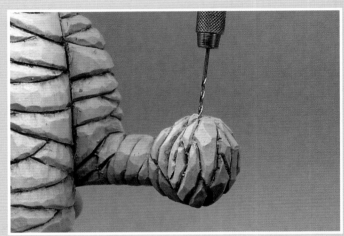

3 Drill a hole in the top of the mummy's hand, as shown.

4 Cut six ½" lengths of 22-gauge black coated wire for the spider legs. Bend the wire in an L shape, as shown. Using cyanoacrylate glue, glue the legs in the holes drilled.

5 Using cyanoacrylate glue, attach a 2" length of black elastic sewing thread in the hole drilled in the spider's head. Glue the remaining end of the elastic in the hole in the mummy's hand.

COLOR CHART

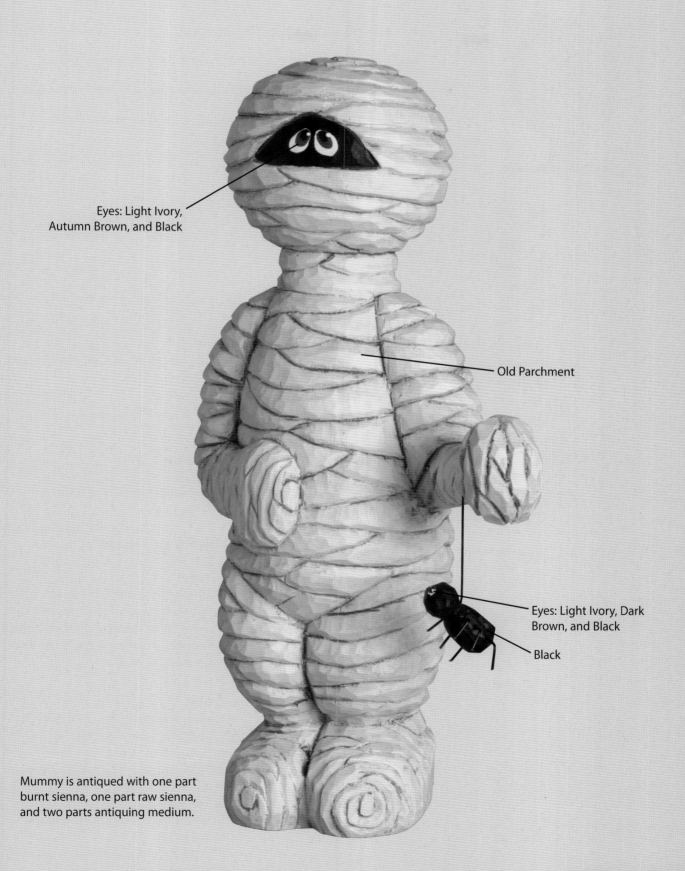

Eyes: Light Ivory, Autumn Brown, and Black

Old Parchment

Eyes: Light Ivory, Dark Brown, and Black

Black

Mummy is antiqued with one part burnt sienna, one part raw sienna, and two parts antiquing medium.

project 3 cat in pumpkins

We all know a black cat crossing your path is supposed to bring bad luck, but this one only brings Happy Halloween wishes. Another figure that's perfect for decorating a tabletop or other surface, this Cat in Pumpkins project will give you practice carving round sections.

tools and supplies

carving
- 3" x 3" x 6" basswood block for pumpkins
- 2" x 2" x 3½" basswood block for cat's head
- Bench knife
- Detail knife
- #3 ⅞" gouge or #3 ⅝" gouge
- #5 3 mm gouge
- #9 5 mm gouge
- Calipers
- Band saw
- Hand drill and ⅟₃₂" drill bit
- Baling wire or ¼" wooden dowel to dowel cat's head to pumpkins
- Six 2" lengths of 24-gauge black coated wire for whiskers
- Cyanoacrylate glue
- Beacon "Quick Grip" All-Purpose Permanent Adhesive

painting
- Acrylic paint, such as Delta Ceramcoat, in the following colors:
    - Apple green
    - Black
    - Dark flesh
    - Ivory
    - Light ivory
    - Tangerine
- Flat brushes in sizes 2 to 8 for blocking color
- #0 or #1 liner brushes for detail painting
- Black fine-line permanent marker

varnishing
- Water-based satin-finish varnish, mixed one part water to one part varnish (see page 31 for application instructions)
- ¾" wash brush or small flat brush for smaller parts

antiquing
- Antiquing medium/retarder, such as Jo Sonja's (see page 32 for antiquing directions)
- Acrylic paint, such as Delta Ceramcoat, in the following colors:
    - Burnt sienna
    - Raw sienna
- Old flat brush
- Soft cloth or old T-shirt
- Cotton swabs

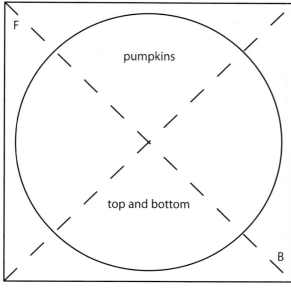

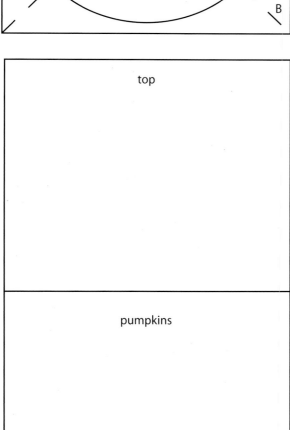

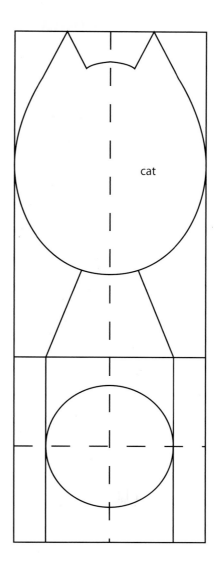

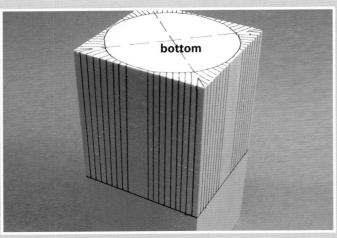

1 Transfer the pattern for the pumpkins to the block. The wood in the shaded area will be removed to create the lower pumpkin.

2 Score the line, as shown, using a bench knife. Use a #3 ⅞" or #3 ⅝" gouge to carve an evenly rounded cylinder.

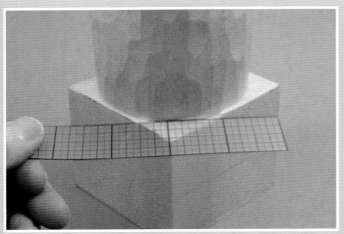

3 The carved cylinder should be ⅝" in from the corners of the block.

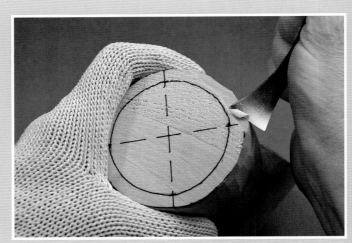

4 Measure in ¼" from the edge of the cylinder, creating a circle. Using the #3 ⅞" or #3 ⅝" gouge, round the lower edge of the pumpkin.

5 Continue rounding the lower edge until it blends well into the sides of the pumpkin. The progress to this point shows the lower pumpkin roughed in.

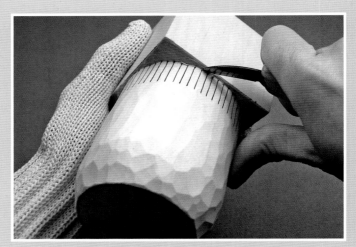

6 Using the bench knife, score the upper edge of the bottom pumpkin, as shown.

7 Using the #3 ⅞" or #3 ⅝" gouge, continue to pull in the top portion of the pumpkin.

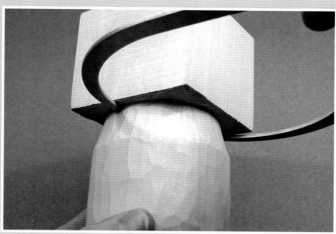

8 Orient the block so the pumpkin is on the bottom, and then measure the top edge diameter with calipers. It should be 2½", or in ¾" from the corners of the upper block and ¼" from the sides. The sides of the top pumpkin bow out and are wider than the top edge of the bottom pumpkin.

9 With the #3 ⅞" or #3 ⅝" gouge, blend the pumpkin to be evenly rounded top to bottom.

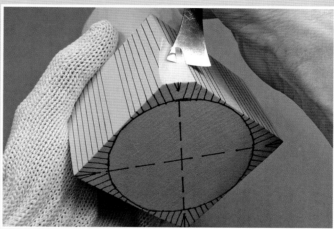

10 The wood in the shaded area will be removed to create the top pumpkin. Use the #3 ⅞" or #3 ⅝" gouge to carve an evenly rounded cylinder.

bottom pumpkin

top pumpkin

11 The cylinder should extend ¼" beyond the lower pumpkin. Note: To measure this, I flip the piece upside down so the bottom pumpkin is on top.

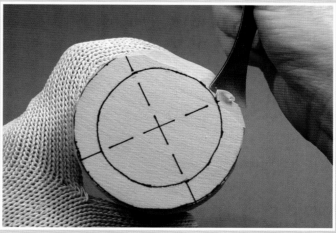

12 Measure in ⅜" from the edge of the top pumpkin, creating a circle. Use the #3 ⅞" or #3 ⅝" gouge to round in to the circle.

13 Blend the pumpkin 1¼" down the sides.

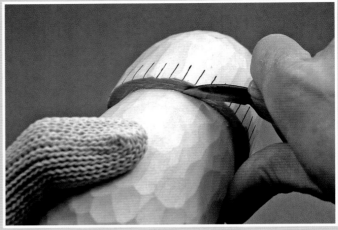

14 Score a line between the pumpkins using the bench knife.

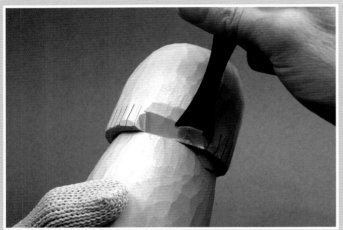

15 Round the top pumpkin down to the scored line with the #3 ⅞" or #3 ⅝" gouge.

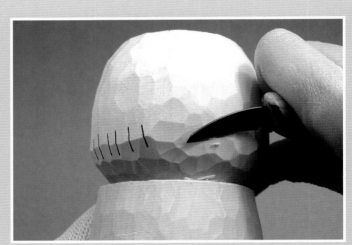

16 Continue to score with the bench knife, and carve back to the scored line until you have created a ⅛" rim on the bottom pumpkin.

17 Make sure the top pumpkin is evenly rounded, as shown here.

18 Divide the circle on the bottom of the lower pumpkin with lines that create six evenly spaced sections. Continue the lines up the sides of the lower pumpkin. Repeat this process on the top pumpkin, staggering the lines from the lower pumpkin.

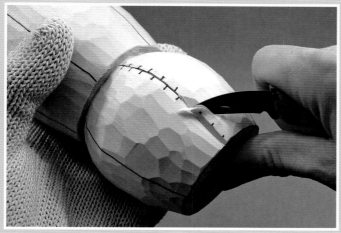

19 Use the bench knife to score each line on the sides of the pumpkins. Carve back to the centerline to add detail to the pumpkins.

20 Draw scary faces on the pumpkins. Note the faces are slightly offset from one another.

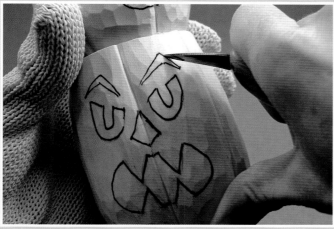

21 With a detail knife, outline all the face lines.

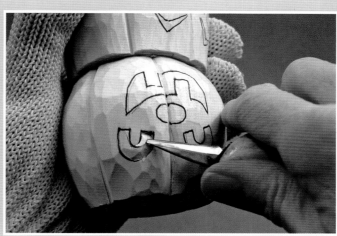

22 Use the detail knife to carve away a small amount of wood inside the face lines. A #5 3 mm gouge also works well for removing wood in narrow spaces.

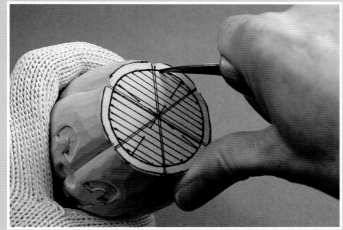

23 Measure in ¼" from the edge of the top pumpkin, creating a circle. Score this line with the bench knife or detail knife.

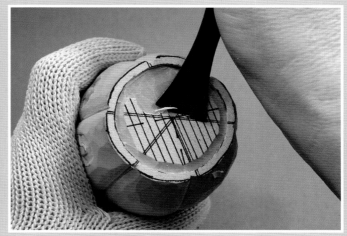

24 Remove a small amount of wood inside the circle with the bench knife and the #3 ⅞" or #3 ⅝" gouge to form a recess ⅛" deep.

25 Round the top edge with the bench knife.

26 Band saw the pattern for the cat's head.

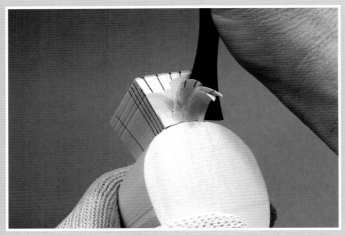

27 With the #3 ⅞" or #3 ⅝" gouge, remove the wood in the shaded area to shape the cat's neck.

28 Use the #3 ⅞" or #3 ⅝" gouge to round the neck. The diameter of the cat's neck at the base is 1" and near the head, ¾".

29 Remove the wood in the shaded area to shape the back of the cat's head.

30 With the #3 ⅞" or #3 ⅝" gouge, carefully round the backs of the ears.

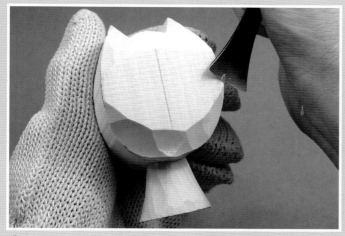

31 Round the wood down to the neck using the #3 ⅞" or #3 ⅝" gouge.

32 Continue to shape the back of the cat's head until it is roughed in, as shown here.

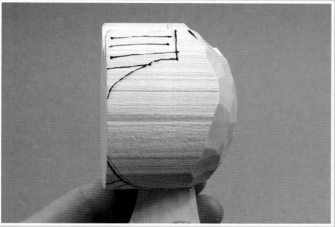

33 Remove the wood in the shaded area to shape the cat's face using the #3 ⅞" or #3 ⅝" gouge.

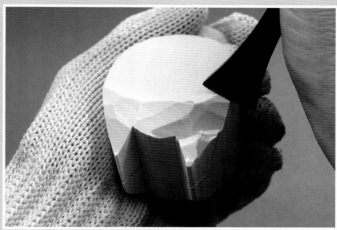

34 Continue to shape the upper part of the cat's face.

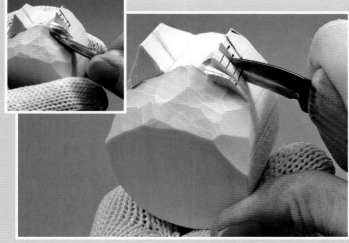

35 Using the bench knife or the detail knife, carve away thin layers as you near the cat's ear line.

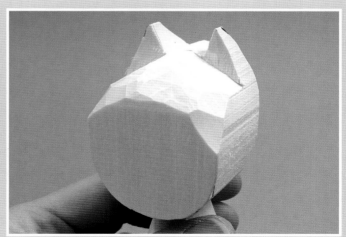

36 Continue carving until the cat's ears are clearly defined. The progress to this point shows the cat's face starting to take shape.

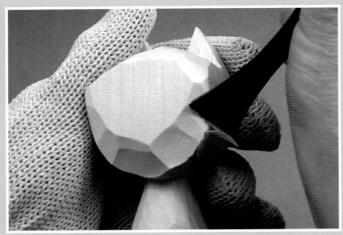

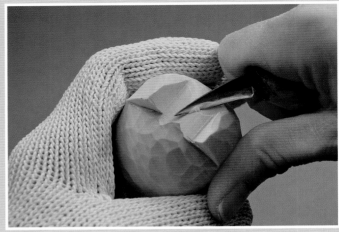

37 Round the lower part of the cat's face into the neck using the #3 ⅞" or #3 ⅝" gouge.

38 With the detail knife, shape between the ears. The cat's face should be evenly rounded, front to back and top to bottom, before you move on to the next step.

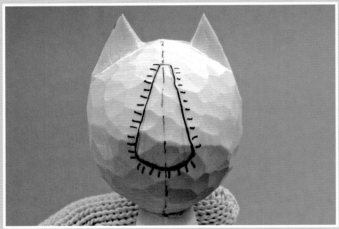

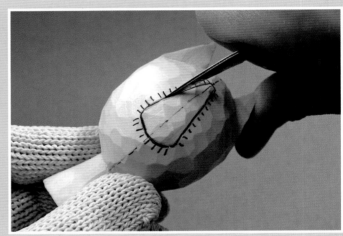

39 Draw in the cat's nose. It starts ⅞" down from the front of the ears. The nose is 1¼" long, ⅝" wide at the bottom, and ⅛" wide at the top.

40 Score the lines around the nose with the detail knife.

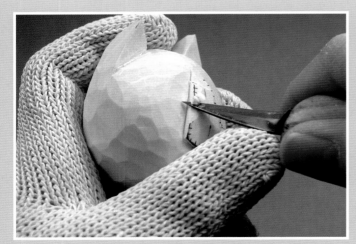

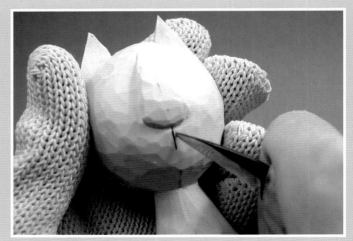

41 With the detail knife, remove wood on the three sides of the nose to ⅛" deep. Then, round the sharp edge.

42 Use the detail knife to score a ⁵⁄₁₆" line below the nose. Remove a sliver of wood on each side of the line to add face detail.

43 Use a #9 5 mm gouge to shape the recessed area of the ears.

44 When the cat's head is finished, as shown, wire or wood dowel the head to the pumpkins (see pages 34–35).

45 The project is now ready to be painted.

painting and finishing

Paint the cat and the pumpkins according to the color chart.
Varnish and antique the carving. Then, follow the instructions in
this section to assemble the project.

1 The base color for the cat's eyes is apple green. Apply the color using the wooden end
of a paintbrush dipped in the paint. This will give you very round, even dots. Redip the
end of the brush for the second eye so the dots will be of equal size. Use a black fine-line
permanent marker to add the cat's pupils. Finish with a sparkle of light ivory.

2 Cut six 2" lengths of 24-gauge black coated wire. Randomly bend and crimp the wire. Using
a hand drill and a ½₂" drill bit, drill three holes (highlighted as orange dots) on each side of
the cat's face. (Note: The orange dots are for reference only and are not actually painted on
the cat's face.) Apply a dot of cyanoacrylate glue to one end of each wire, and insert the
wires into the holes. Bend the wires to achieve the desired effect.

COLOR CHART

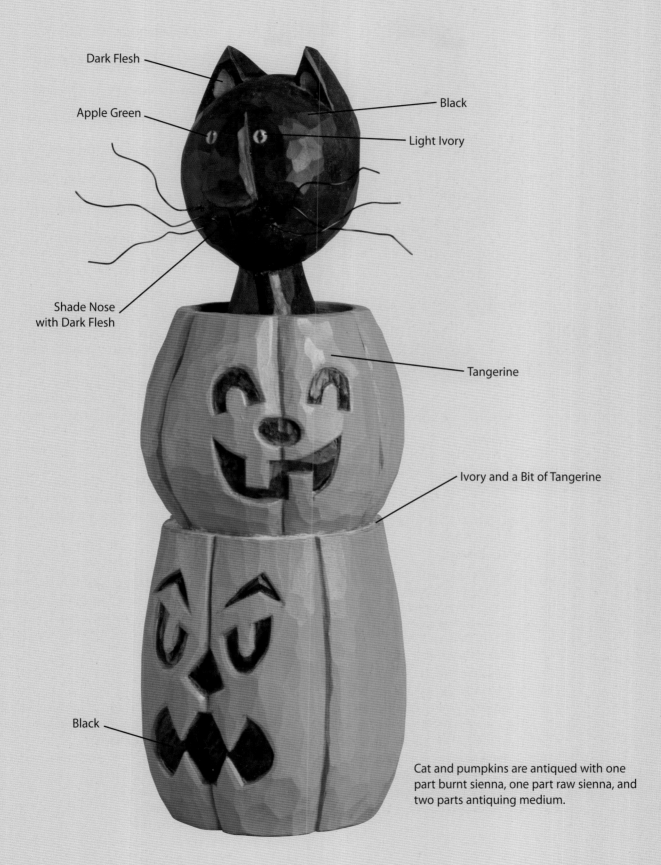

Dark Flesh

Apple Green

Black

Light Ivory

Shade Nose
with Dark Flesh

Tangerine

Ivory and a Bit of Tangerine

Black

Cat and pumpkins are antiqued with one
part burnt sienna, one part raw sienna, and
two parts antiquing medium.

project 4 ghost trick-or-treaters

Aside from being great additions to your Halloween décor, these two trick-or-treaters illustrate how small modifications can create a new project. With one trick-or-treater, the side with the outstretched arm has been reversed and the shoes have been changed. I'll show you the steps for each in this demonstration.

tools and supplies

carving
- Two 3" x 3" x 6" basswood blocks for bodies
- Two 1¼" x 1¼" x 1¼" basswood blocks for arms
- Two 1¼" x 1¼" x 1¼" basswood blocks for jack o'lanterns
- Four ⅞" x 1¾" x 1¼" blocks for shoes
- Bench knife
- Detail knife
- #3 ⅞" gouge or #3 ⅝" gouge
- #9 10 mm gouge
- #5 3 mm gouge
- #9 5 mm gouge
- 1 mm V-tool
- #11 1 mm micro tool
- Hand drill and 1⁄16" drill bit
- Needle-nose pliers
- Baling wire to dowel arms to bodies
- 3⁄16" wooden dowel to dowel legs to bodies
- Four 1¼" length 20-gauge black coated wire for jack o'lantern handles
- Cyanoacrylate glue
- Beacon "Quick Grip" All-Purpose Permanent Adhesive

painting
- Acrylic paint, such as Delta Ceramcoat, in the following colors:

Autumn brown	Black
Blue heaven	Dark brown
Light ivory	Medium flesh
Metallic gold	Nightfall
Persimmon	Sandstone
Santa's flesh	Tangerine
Tomato spice	Wedgewood blue

- Flat brushes in sizes 2 to 8 for blocking color
- #0 or #1 liner brushes for detail painting
- Stylus

varnishing
- Water-based satin-finish varnish, mixed one part water to one part varnish (see page 31 for application instructions)
- ¾" wash brush or small flat brush for smaller parts

antiquing
- Antiquing medium/retarder, such as Jo Sonja's (see page 32 for antiquing directions)
- Acrylic paint, such as Delta Ceramcoat, in the following colors:
  Burnt sienna
  Raw sienna
- Old flat brush
- Soft cloth or old T-shirt
- Cotton swabs

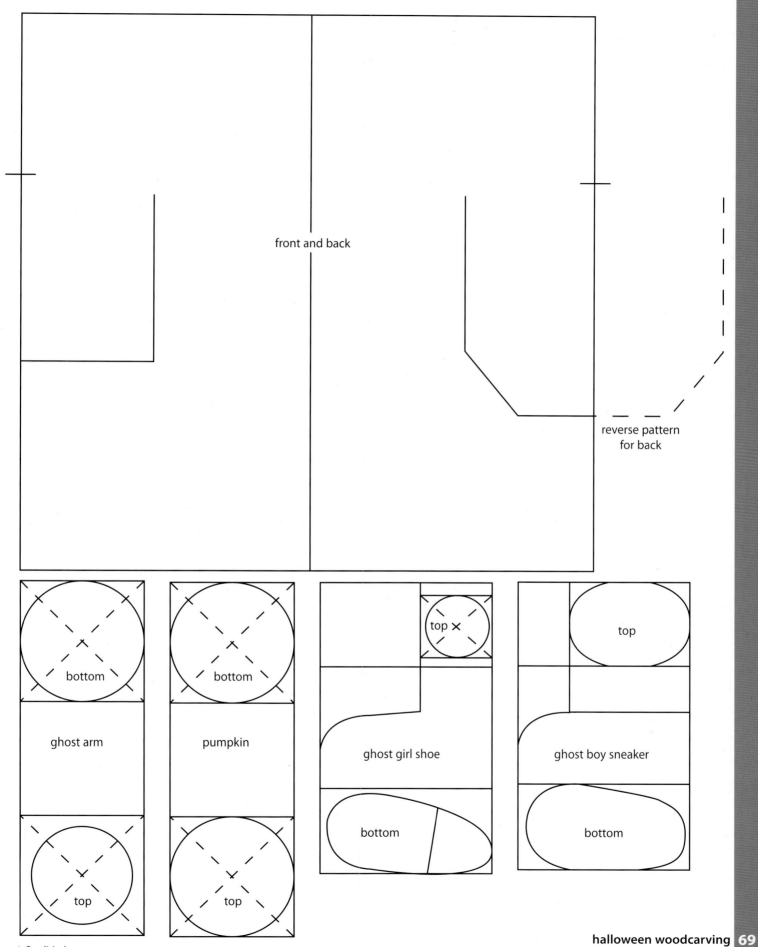

front and back

reverse pattern
for back

bottom

ghost arm

top

bottom

pumpkin

top

top ✕

ghost girl shoe

bottom

top

ghost boy sneaker

bottom

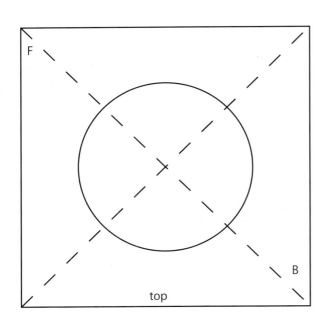

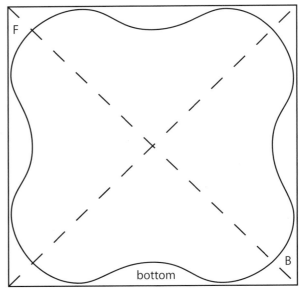

© Cyndi Joslyn

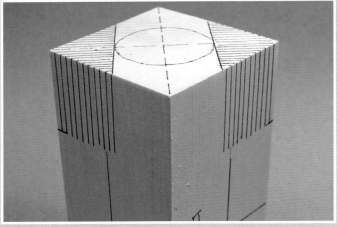

1 Transfer the pattern to one of the blocks for the body, as shown, for the girl trick-or-treater. Reverse the pattern for the boy trick-or-treater.

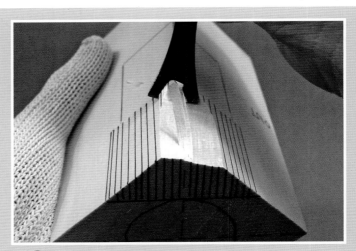

2 At the shoulder mark, use a #3 ⅞" or #3 ⅝" gouge to begin removing wood with a curved, scooping motion.

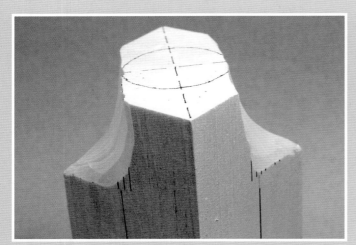

3 Continue removing wood to form the shoulders. Notice there is no sharp angle above the shoulder.

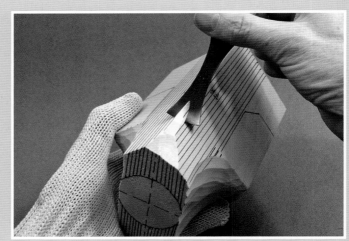

4 Using the #3 ⅞" or #3 ⅝" gouge, round the wood in the shaded area up to the circle on top of the ghost on the front and on the back.

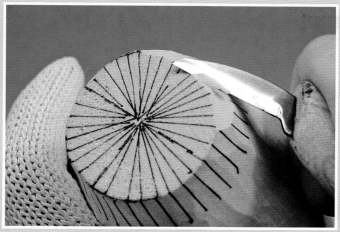

5 Evenly round the top of the head using the #3 ⅞" or #3 ⅝" gouge and a bench knife.

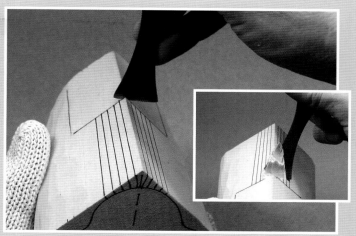

6 Make a stop cut under the elbow, and remove the wood in the shaded area under the elbow to the edge of the pattern on the bottom of the ghost.

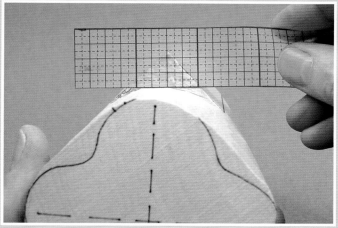

7 Remove wood to a depth of ⅝" from the lower corner of the elbow.

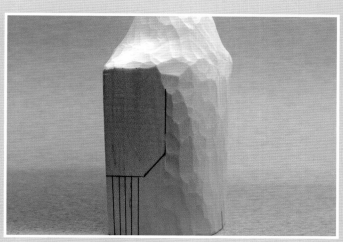

8 Remove the wood in the shaded area under the right arm.

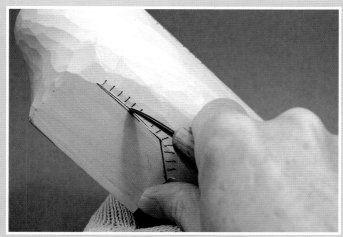

9 Remove the wood in the shaded area to define the arms by first making a stop cut with a bench knife.

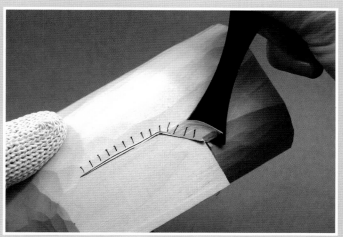

10 Use the #3 ⅞" or #3 ⅝" gouge to remove the wood up to the stop cut.

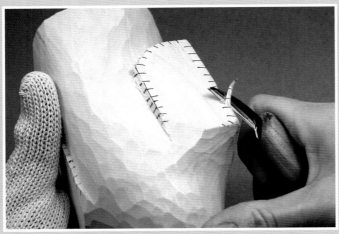

11 Round the edges of the arms with the bench knife.

12 Start 1⅜" above the bottom and, using a #9 10 mm gouge, carve rounded trenches to add curves to the bottom of the ghost's costume.

13 Round the edges of these curves with the detail knife.

14 Transfer the lower arm pattern to the top and bottom of the block for the arm. Make one for each of the trick-or-treaters. Use the #3 ⅞" or #3 ⅝" gouge to carve away wood to create an evenly rounded cylinder.

15 Remove the wood in the shaded area to refine the arm. Use the bench knife to evenly round the end of the lower arm.

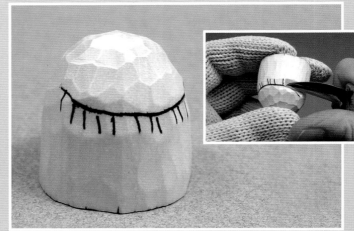

16 Draw the hand line, as shown. Then, score and remove a small amount of wood in the shaded area with the bench knife.

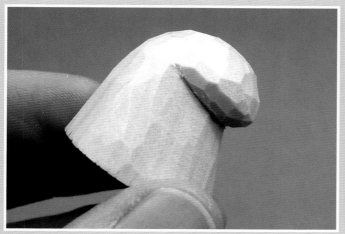

17 Round the sharp edge with the bench knife or a detail knife,

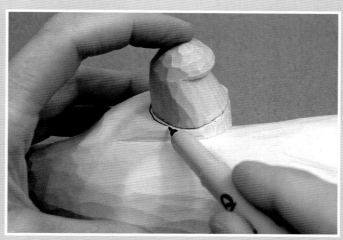

18 Position the lower arm on the upper arm and trace the desired position.

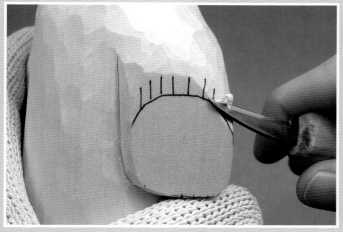

19 Using the bench knife, round the upper arm above where the lower arm will be attached.

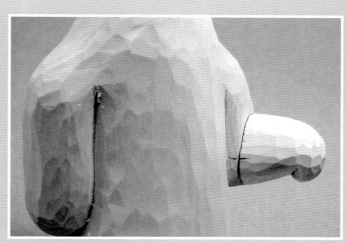

20 Attach the lower arm using the wire dowel technique (see page 35). Blend the arm sections with the bench knife.

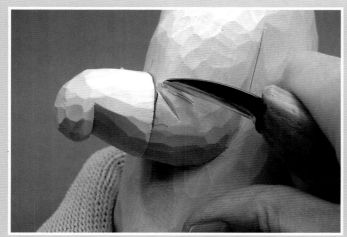

21 Draw crease lines on the outside and inside of the elbow. Score the lines and remove a thin wedge of wood on each side of these lines using the bench knife.

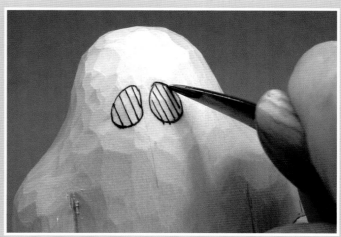

22 Draw the eye holes, as shown. The eye holes are approximately ⅜" wide and ½" long. Use the detail knife to score the outline of the eye holes.

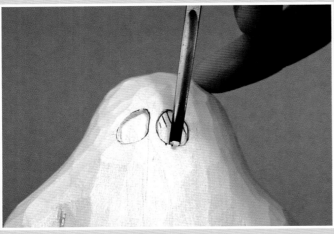

23 Use the detail knife and a #5 3 mm gouge to remove a small amount of wood in the shaded area.

24 Transfer the pumpkin pattern to the top and bottom of the blocks for the jack o' lanterns.

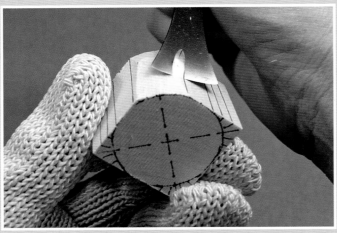

25 Round the sides of each block outside the circles on the top and bottom using the #3 7/8" or #3 5/8" gouge. Carve an evenly rounded cylinder.

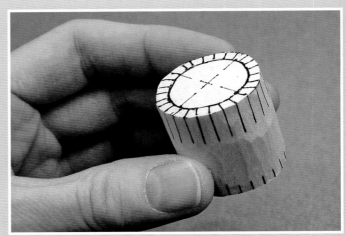

26 Measure in 1/8" from the edge on the top of the pumpkin. Round the pumpkin in a fashion similar to that used in the Cat in Pumpkins project (see Steps 13–17 on page 60).

27 Continue to add details in a fashion similar to that used in the Cat in Pumpkins project (see Steps 20–25 on page 61–62).

28 Transfer the pattern to the sides, top, and bottom of the block for the girl's right shoe. Reverse the pattern for the left shoe on a separate block.

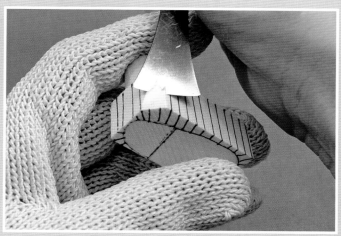

29 Remove the wood in the shaded area on the top section of the shoe. Use the #3 ⅞" or #3 ⅝" gouge to carve an evenly rounded cylinder, as shown.

30 Use the #3 ⅞" or #3 ⅝" gouge to remove the wood in the shaded area to shape the sides of the shoe, as shown.

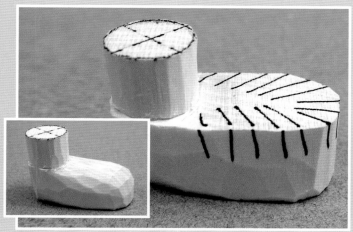

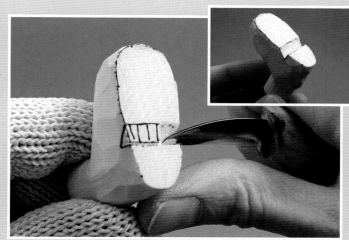

31 Continue rounding the toe area of the shoe with the #3 ⅞" or #3 ⅝" gouge.

32 With the bench knife, score a deep line on the bottom of the shoe. Remove the wood in the shaded area in an angled fashion, as shown.

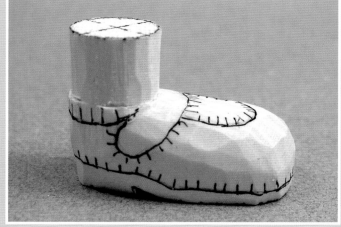

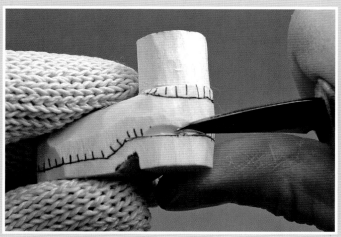

33 Draw the shoe details, as shown. Remember to reverse the pattern for the left shoe.

34 Using the detail knife, score the sole line and remove a small amount of wood above the score line. Round the sharp edge.

35 Score around the top shoe detail with the detail knife, and then use the #5 3 mm gouge to remove a small amount of wood on the top detail.

36 Draw a line ⅜" down from the top of the leg. Use a #9 5 mm gouge to score a scalloped edge on this line, creating the anklet. Apply enough pressure to the gouge to score the wood at least ¹⁄₁₆" deep.

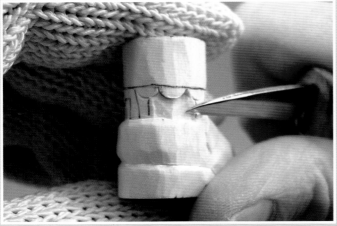

37 Use the detail knife to remove a small amount of wood between the edge of the anklet and the shoe.

38 Here is the finished shoe. Notice that all of the parts have been defined and all edges of the shoe slightly rounded.

39 Transfer the pattern to the sides, top, and bottom of the block for the boy's right sneaker. Reverse the pattern for the left sneaker on a separate block.

40 Use the #3 ⅞" or #3 ⅝" gouge to carve an evenly rounded, oblong cylinder that will be the cuff above the sneaker. Score under the cuff with the bench knife.

41 Using the #3 ⅞" or #3 ⅝" gouge, remove the wood in the shaded area to shape the sides of the sneaker.

42 Use the #3 ⅞" or #3 ⅝" gouge to shape the sides of the sneaker, pull the sneaker under the cuff, and round the top of the sneaker.

43 Draw the details of the sneaker, as shown. Remove a small amount of wood in the shaded areas with the detail knife.

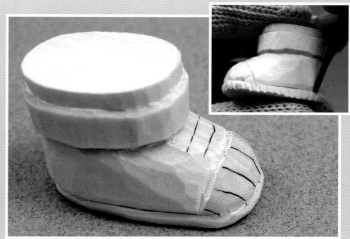

44 Carve the lace lines and add detail to the toe of the sneaker with a 1 mm V-tool. Use a #11 1 mm micro tool to add detail to the sole of the sneaker.

45 This shows the finished sneaker. Notice that all of the parts have been defined and slightly rounded.

46 Dry fit the feet to the body with the wooden dowel technique (see page 34). Do not glue the feet to the body until after they are painted.

painting and finishing

Paint, antique, and varnish the project using the colors listed in the supplies list and following the color chart. Then, follow the instructions found in this section for assembling the trick-or-treaters.

COLOR CHART

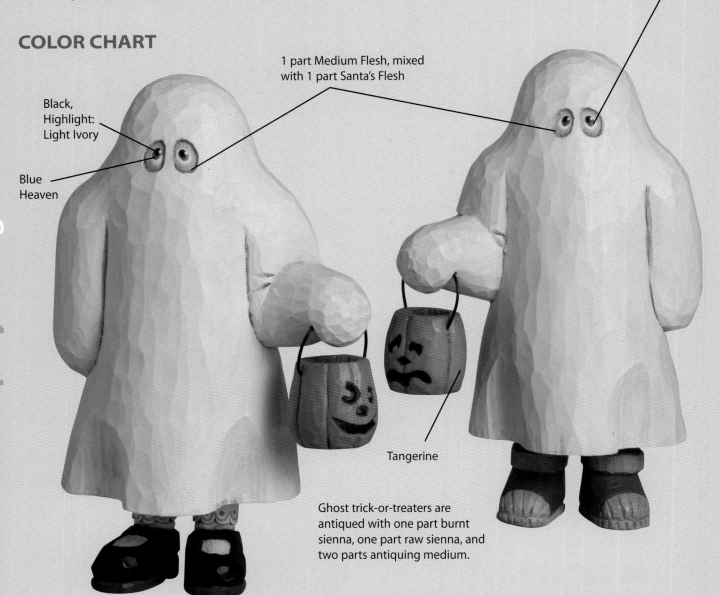

Autumn Brown

Black, Highlight: Light Ivory

1 part Medium Flesh, mixed with 1 part Santa's Flesh

Blue Heaven

Tangerine

Ghost trick-or-treaters are antiqued with one part burnt sienna, one part raw sienna, and two parts antiquing medium.

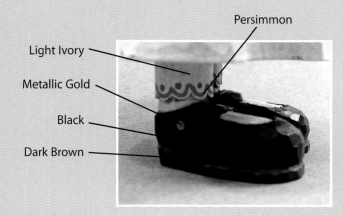

Persimmon

Light Ivory

Metallic Gold

Black

Dark Brown

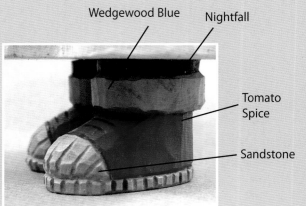

Wedgewood Blue

Nightfall

Tomato Spice

Sandstone

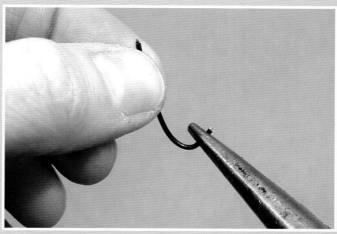

1 Once you have painted the rest of the ghosts, paint the eyes. Be sure to allow the paint to thoroughly dry between all steps. With a liner brush, paint angled ovals in light ivory. Add the iris color. Blue heaven is a good choice for blue eyes; autumn brown, for brown eyes. Add black for pupils. The final step is to add tiny dots of light ivory for the sparkles. Add the dot with a stylus; place it on the right side of the right eye and also on the right side of the left eye. The positioning makes it appear as if there is one light source being reflected in the eyes.

2 Cut two lengths of 20-gauge black coated wire 1¼" long. Use needle-nose pliers to bend a right angle ¼" from one end of each wire.

3 Use a hand drill and a ¹⁄₁₆" drill bit to drill ¼" holes in each side of the pumpkin, as shown. Apply a dot of cyanoacrylate glue to the bent end of the wire, and insert that end into the drilled hole on each side.

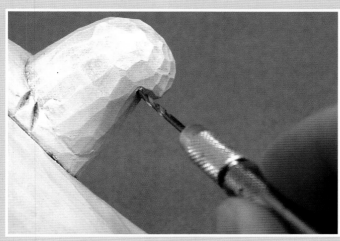

4 Drill holes ¼" deep on the inside and outside of the ghost's hand, as shown.

5 Dry fit the wires into the holes in the hands. Trim the wire as needed so the jack o' lantern hangs evenly. Apply dots of cyanoacrylate glue to the wire ends, and insert the ends in the holes in the hand.

project 5 witch

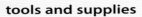

What's Halloween without a witch? For this project, I've chosen a witch who's holding a wand and a crow, and I've also given her a straight, pointed hat. However, I've also given you the option to carve this witch holding a quilt or wearing a crooked hat. When you come to the hand or hat carving parts in the demonstration, you can simply substitute the hand or hat that fits the carving you want to create.

tools and supplies

carving
- 2½" x 2½" x 7¼" basswood block for body
- Two 1" x 1" x 1¾" basswood blocks for arms
- 1½" x 1½" x 3" basswood block for top of witch's hat
- Two ¾" x 2½" x 2⅛" basswood blocks for boots
- ¾" x ¾" x 2⅛" basswood block for crow
  - Graphite paper
  - Transparent tape
  - Stylus
  - Bench knife
- Detail knife
- #3 ⅞" gouge or #3 ⅝" gouge
- #9 10 mm gouge
- #11 3 mm gouge
- #8 7 mm gouge
- 1 mm V-tool
- Band saw
- Scroll saw
- Hand drill and 1⁄16" drill bit
- Round toothpick for crow's beak
- Found twig for witch's wand
- Baling wire to dowel arms to body, top of hat to bottom, and wand to hand
- 3⁄16" wooden dowel to dowel legs to body
- 1" length of 20-gauge black coated wire to dowel crow to hand
- Cyanoacrylate glue
- Carpenter's wood filler

painting
- Acrylic paint, such as Delta Ceramcoat, in the following colors:

Apple green	Autumn brown
Black	Charcoal
Cricket	Dark brown
Lichen grey	Light ivory
Magnolia white	Passion
Pumpkin	Quaker grey
Tangerine	

- Flat brushes in sizes 2 to 8 for blocking color
- #0 or #1 liner brushes for detail painting
- Black extrafine-line permanent marker

varnishing
- Water-based satin-finish varnish, mixed one part water to one part varnish (see page 31 for application instructions)
- ¾" wash brush or small flat brush for smaller parts

antiquing
- Antiquing medium/retarder, such as Jo Sonja's (see page 32 for antiquing directions)
- Acrylic paint, such as Delta Ceramcoat, in the following colors:
  - Burnt sienna
  - Raw sienna
- Old flat brush
- Soft cloth or old T-shirt
- Cotton swabs

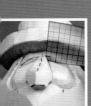

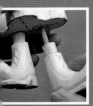

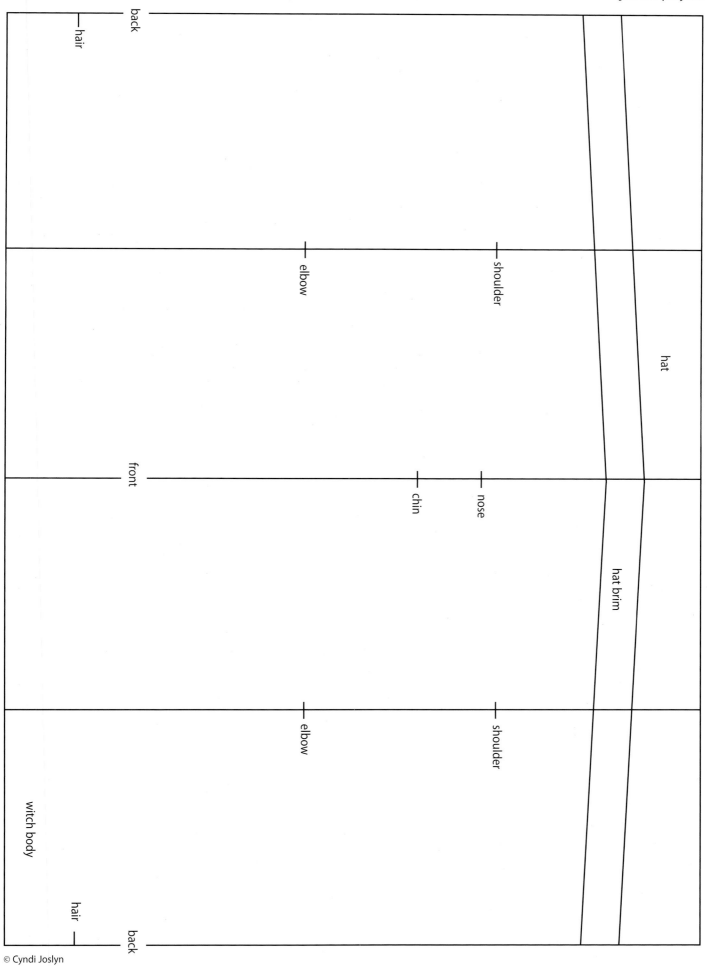

back
hair

elbow

shoulder

hat

front

chin

nose

hat brim

elbow

shoulder

witch body

hair

back

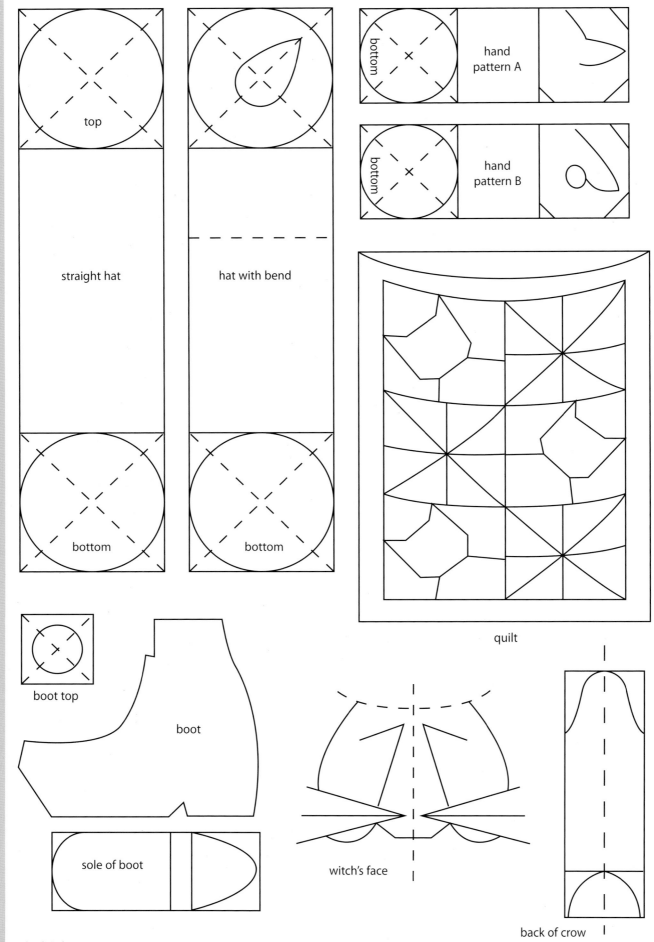

top

bottom

hand pattern A

bottom

hand pattern B

straight hat

hat with bend

bottom

bottom

quilt

boot top

boot

sole of boot

witch's face

back of crow

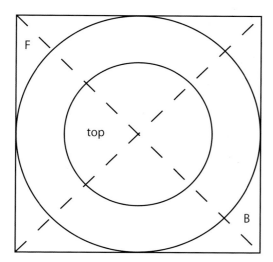

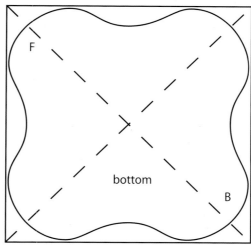

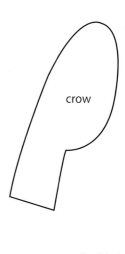

crow

© Cyndi Joslyn

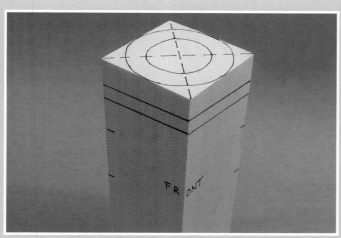

1 Transfer the body pattern to the block for the body.

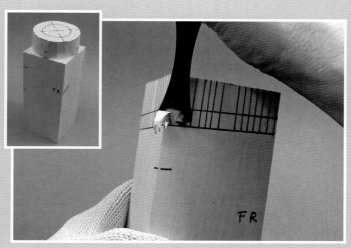

2 Using a bench knife and a #3 ⅞" or #3 ⅝" gouge, remove the wood in the shaded area to produce an evenly rounded cylinder.

3 From the base, measure up ⅜" at several points around the cylinder. Connect the points to form a line.

4 The wood in the shaded area will be removed to form the base of the witch's hat. Remove the wood using the bench knife and the #3 ⅞" or #3 ⅝" gouge to form a smaller, evenly rounded cylinder.

halloween woodcarving 83

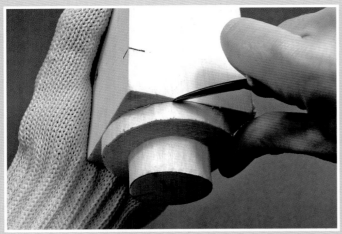

5 Score under the rim of the hat, as shown, using the bench knife.

6 Use the #3 ⅞" or #3 ⅝" gouge to score the tops of the shoulders.

7 Carve back to the shoulder with the #3 ⅞" or #3 ⅝" gouge. Remove wood to a depth of ½" from the point of the shoulder.

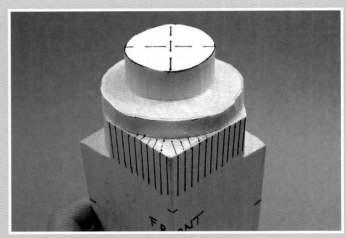

8 The wood in the shaded area will be rounded as preliminary shaping of the witch's face.

9 Carve back to the hat brim with the #3 ⅞" or #3 ⅝" gouge to shape the face, as shown.

10 The wood in the shaded area will be rounded as preliminary shaping for the witch's hair. Carve back under the hat, as shown, with the #3 ⅞" or #3 ⅝" gouge.

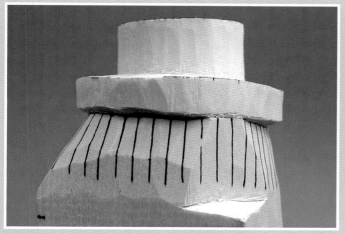

11 Use the #3 ⅞" or #3 ⅝" gouge to remove the wood in the shaded area to further define the witch's head.

12 Continue to score under the brim with the bench knife and remove wood with the #3 ⅞" or #3 ⅝" gouge. . .

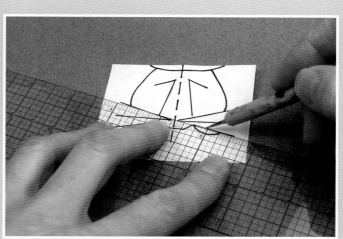

13 . . . until the lower brim measures ⅜" deep and the face area is evenly rounded. Redraw the centerline on the face, as shown.

14 Trace the witch's face pattern onto a piece of paper. With the pattern on a hard surface, use the stylus to score the three lines on each side of the nose, as shown.

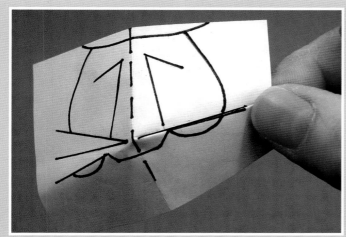

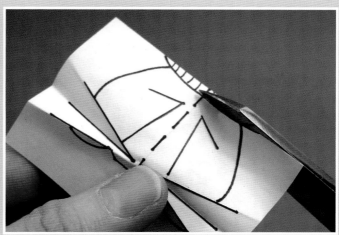

15 Fold darts in the face pattern to shape the pattern to fit the contour of the wood.

16 Cut away the shaded area, as shown.

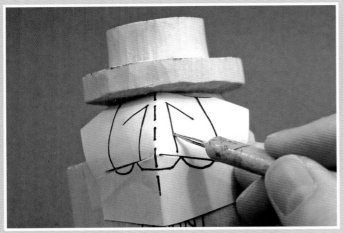

17 Center the pattern under the carved brim of the hat, matching the registration lines. Sandwich a small piece of graphite paper between the pattern and the wood, shiny side toward the wood. Use two small pieces of transparent tape to hold the darts in place and the pattern on the wood. Trace the face pattern onto the wood using the stylus.

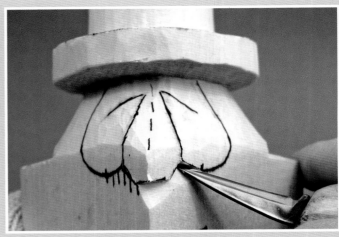

18 Score the line between the points, as shown, with a detail knife. Remove a small amount of wood under the line, as shown.

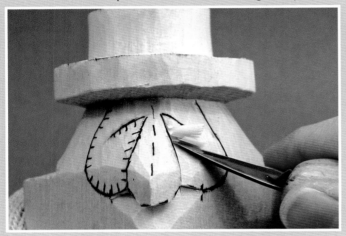

19 With the detail knife, score the remaining face lines and remove wood around the nose, under the eyebrows, and around the cheeks, as shown.

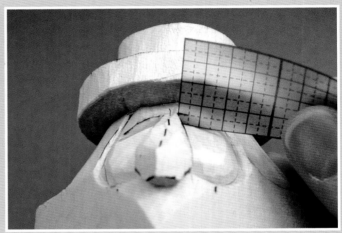

20 Make sure the depth of the cheeks under each eyebrow is ⅛".

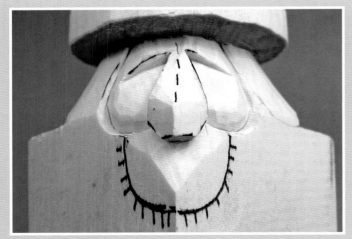

21 Draw the chin, as shown. The point of the chin is about ⅝" below the nose.

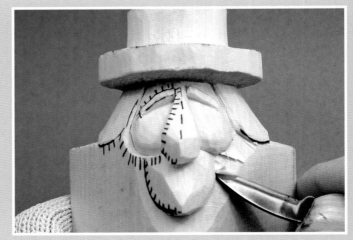

22 Score around the chin and remove a small amount of wood, as shown, using the bench knife.

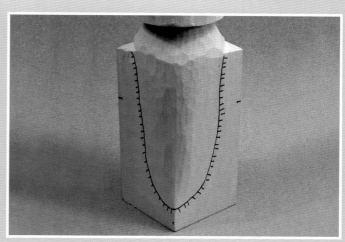

23 Draw the eyebrows and remove a small amount of wood around each eyebrow for definition. Pull in wood under the cheeks, as shown. Round the lower chin. Round the sides of the nose. Pull the shoulder in under the hair. Refer back to the photo in Step 22 to see where wood is removed.

24 Draw in the hair outline.

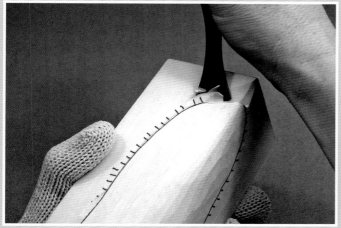

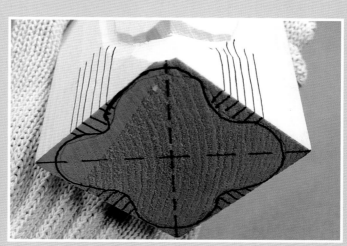

25 Score the lines with a bench knife and remove wood with a #3 ⅞" or #3 ⅝" gouge, as shown, to define the hair outline.

26 The wood in the shaded areas will be removed to add curves to the skirt.

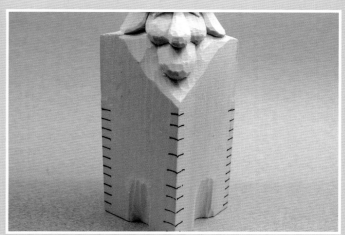

27 Use a #9 10 mm gouge to carve the curves in the skirt. The curves extend 1½" up from the base on the front of the skirt and 1¼" on the back of the skirt.

28 Wood in shaded areas will be removed to further shape the witch's body.

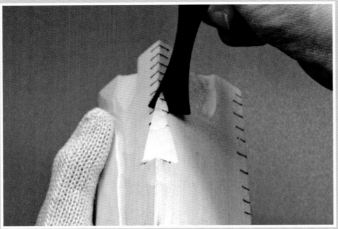

29 Use the #3 7/8" or #3 5/8" gouge to create a stop cut at the elbow. Round the sides of the skirt up under the elbow. Round in to a depth of 3/8" from the point of the elbow.

30 Round the front of the witch from the bottom of the skirt to under the witch's chin using the #3 7/8" or #3 5/8" gouge.

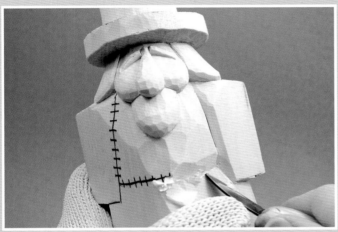

31 Draw in the waist and the sides of the arms as follows: The waist is 3½" up from the base of the skirt. Measure in 1" from the edge of the wood at the elbow, and then connect the line up to the hairline, as shown, to define the arms. Score lines and carve back to define the waist and the arms with the bench knife.

32 Continue carving until the waist and the insides of the arms are clearly defined. The progress to this point shows the details of the witch's face with the rest of the body starting to take shape.

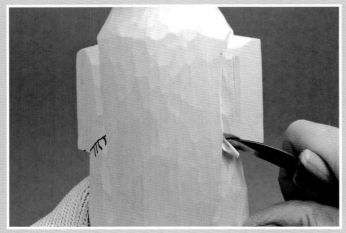

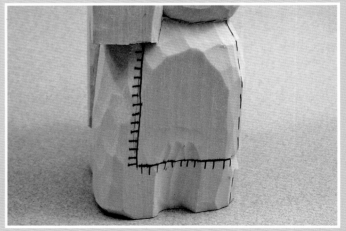

33 Draw a line from the elbow to the hair, as shown. Score the wood with the bench knife and remove the wood under the elbow to define it using the #3 7/8" or #3 5/8" gouge.

34 Draw the centerline on the skirt front. To create the apron, measure up 1" from the base of the skirt to establish the bottom edge of the apron and make a mark. Measure out 1¾" on each side of the centerline to establish the sides of the apron. Draw the lines marking the bottom and sides of the apron, as shown.

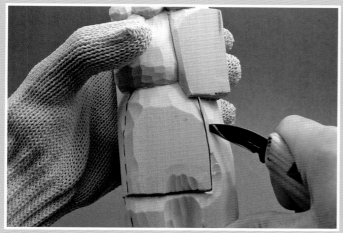

35 Score the apron lines with the bench knife and begin shaping the apron as shown.

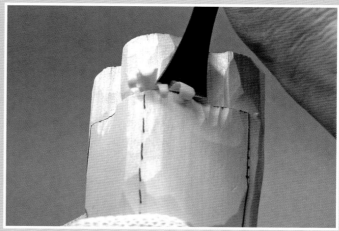

36 Continue to remove wood, as shown, outside the apron to define it using the #3 ⅞" or #3 ⅝" gouge.

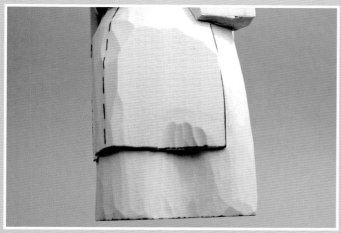

37 Using the #9 10 mm gouge, continue the curve of the skirt up 1" on the bottom edge of the apron, as shown.

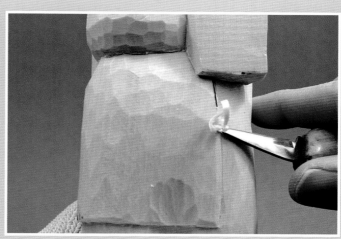

38 Round the edges of the apron with the detail knife.

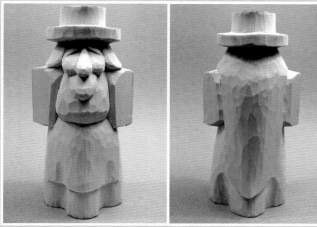

39 The progress to this point illustrates the witch with her apron and curved skirt.

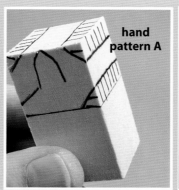

hand pattern A

Making a Witch Holding a Quilt

As an alternative to the wand and the crow, you can opt to make this witch holding a quilt. Simply make a right and left hand using hand pattern A. For more detailed instructions, see pages 102–105.

40 Transfer the patterns for the arms to the blocks of wood sized for the arms. The left hand (shown) will hold the crow (hand pattern A). The right hand will hold the wand (hand pattern B). If you decide to make the witch with the quilt, use pattern A for both hands. You'll simply need to reverse the pattern for the right hand. The wood in the shaded area will be removed.

halloween woodcarving 89

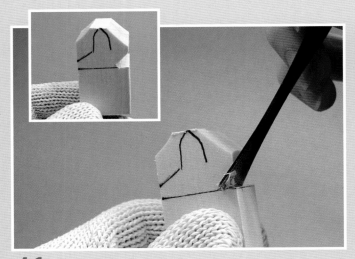

41 Remove the wood to create very flat planes on both hands using the #3 ⅞" or #3 ⅝" gouge. This is a unique time when carving flat is important.

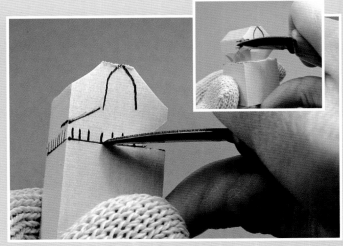

42 Score around the base of each hand and remove a small amount of wood to shape the wrists. The shaping of the wrist is round.

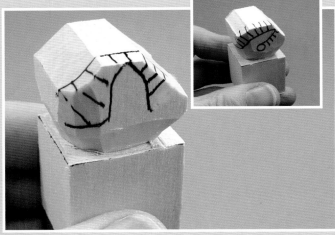

43 Shade the wood on each hand that will be removed to define the thumb. The right hand pattern A is shown in the main photo, and the right hand pattern B is shown in the inset.

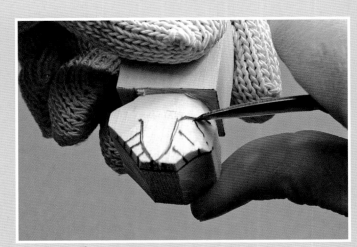

44 Score around the thumb with the bench knife.

45 Remove the wood around the thumb to a depth of ¼".

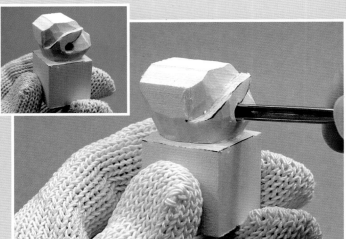

46 For the right hand (pattern B), which holds the wand, use a #11 3 mm gouge and a twisting motion to drill a ⅜" hole to hold the wand.

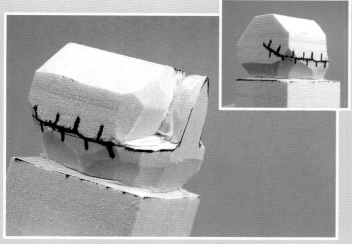

47 Continue the line on the left side of the thumb, as shown. This will identify where the fingers meet the palm.

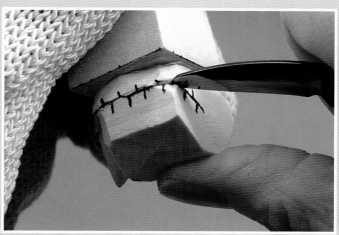

48 Using the bench knife, score the line and remove a small amount of wood on each side of the line to form a shallow trench.

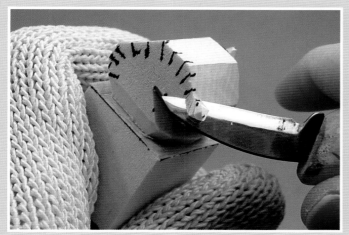

49 Round the edge of the wood on the side of the hand opposite the thumb using the bench knife.

50 Be sure to keep four distinct planes on the hand as shown. The progress to this point shows the different planes that form the hand.

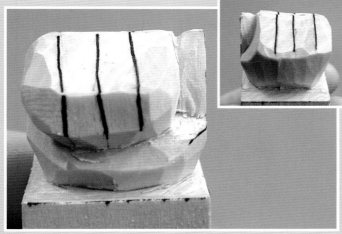

51 Draw in the finger lines, as shown. Starting at the top of the back of the hand, they will extend across the other three planes of the hand.

52 With the detail knife, score each line and remove a sliver of wood as shown on each separate plane to define the fingers between the knuckles.

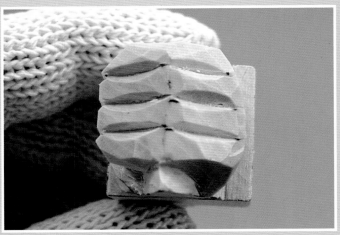

53 The progress to this point illustrates the detail added to the hands. Notice how much wood was removed to define the fingers, and very little to define the knuckles.

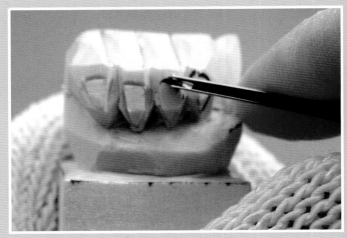

54 Draw the fingernails, and outline them with a 1 mm V-tool.

55 Use the 1 mm V-tool to add knuckle marks at each joint, as shown.

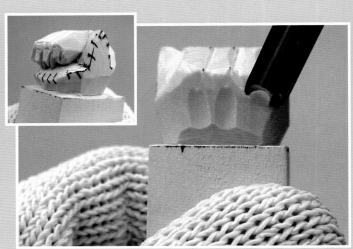

56 Use a #8 7 mm gouge to carve three definition marks in the back of each hand. With the detail knife, round and shape the sides of the thumb and under the fingers.

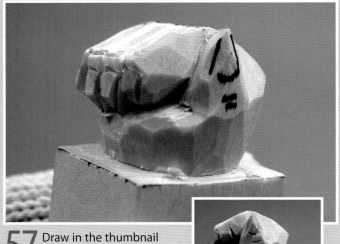

57 Draw in the thumbnail and knuckle marks on the thumb, and outline them with the 1 mm V-tool.

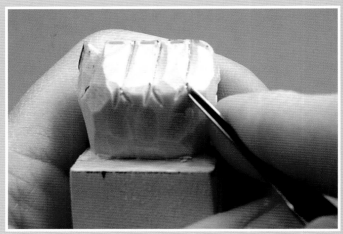

58 Use the 1 mm V-tool to add crease marks to the base of each finger on the back of the hand.

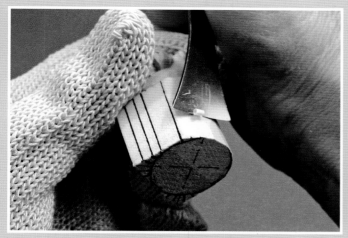

59 Using the #3 ⅞" or #3 ⅝" gouge, remove the wood in the shaded area to create the sleeve. Remove the wood outside the circle and up the length of the sleeve, shaping an evenly rounded cylinder.

60 Slightly round the sharp edge at the top of the sleeve with the detail knife.

61 Here is the finished arm. Note the crease lines in the fingers and the rounded sleeve.

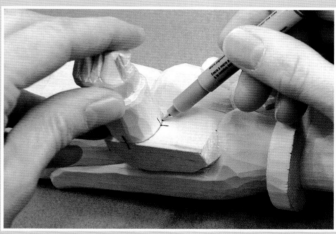

62 Position the witch's lower arm on the upper arm next to the elbow, thumbs up. Trace the desired position of the lower arm onto the upper arm. Mark both arm circumferences at 12, 3, 6, and 9. Connect the vertical and horizontal points to identify the center points on each arm section.

63 Use the #3 ⅞" or #3 ⅝" gouge to round the wood in the shaded area to shape the top and sides of the arm.

64 Wire dowel the arm segments to the body (see page 35).

65 Blend the two segments of the arm together with the #3 ⅞" or #3 ⅝" gouge.

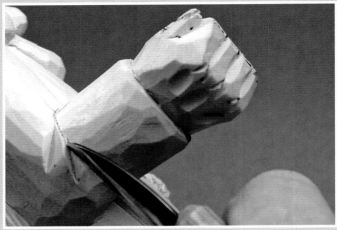

66 With the detail knife, add crease marks on the inside and outside of the elbows.

67 Transfer the boot pattern to ¾" stock for the boots. Band saw the boot outline. This will be the right boot. Reverse the pattern for the left boot. Transfer the pattern to the top of the boots.

68 Remove the wood in the shaded area to shape the leg using a bench knife.

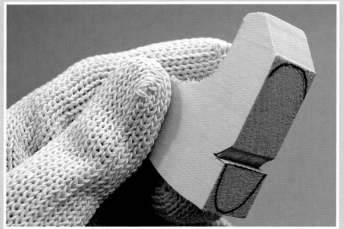

69 Score the line deeply on the bottom of the boot, and remove an angled wedge to a depth of ¼" next to the heel.

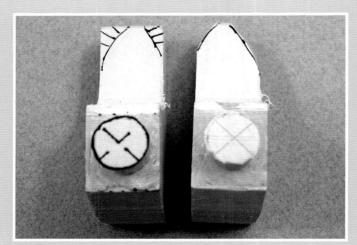

70 Draw the toe lines, and remove the wood in the shaded area to shape.

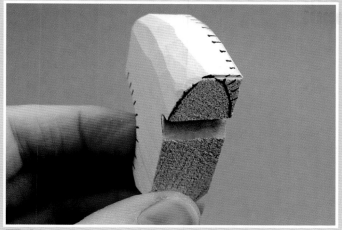

71 Round the edges of the boots with the bench knife.

72 Continue to refine the shape of the boot. The bench knife or detail knife is most handy when carving the curved slope on the toes of the boots.

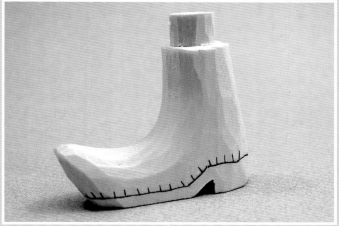

73 Draw the sole line. Then, with the detail knife, score and remove a thin wedge of wood above the sole line. With the detail knife, slightly round the sharp edge on the boot sole.

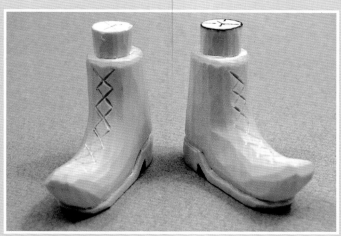

74 With the 1 mm V-tool, add lace marks to complete the boots.

75 Position the legs on the centerline on the bottom of the witch's body, as shown.

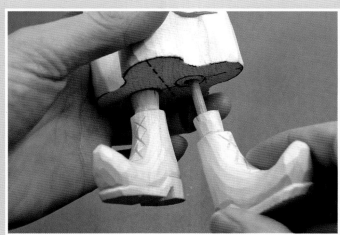

76 Using a ³⁄₁₆" dowel, wood dowel the legs to the body (see page 34). Do not glue the boots in place until after they are painted.

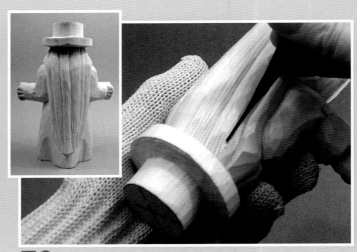

77 Divide the witch's hair into several sections, as shown. With the bench knife, score lines and remove the wood on both sides of the lines to form shallow trenches.

78 Using the 1 mm V-tool, add hair lines to fill in each of the sections.

79 Draw in a crooked smile, as shown. Use the 1 mm V-tool to outline the witch's smile.

80 Transfer the straight hat pattern to the wood. The wood in the shaded area will be removed.

Making a Witch with a Crooked Hat

If you would prefer, you can make a witch with a crooked hat instead of the straight hat shown here. For instructions, see pages 100–101.

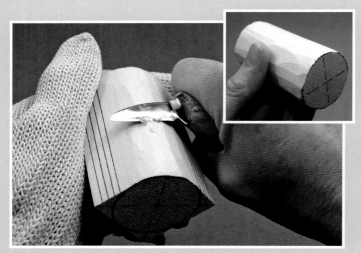

81 Carve away the wood outside of the circle to form an evenly rounded cylinder.

82 Continue to carve wood away at the top of the cylinder to begin to form a cone.

83 Continue to refine the straight hat to complete it.

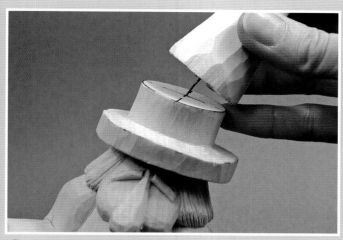

84 Wire dowel the witch's hat sections together (see page 35).

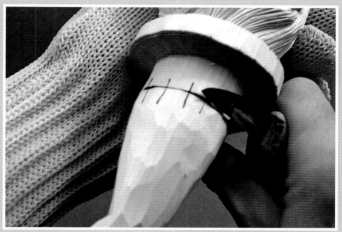

85 Blend the hat sections together using the bench knife.

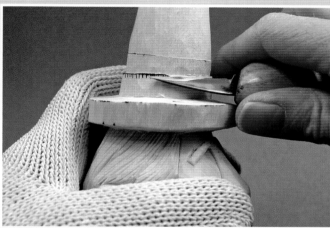

86 Measure up ⅜" from the base of the hat, and mark around the hat at several points. Draw a line to attach the points. With the detail knife, score the line and remove a small amount of wood above the line to form the hatband. Then, slightly round the sharp edge of the hatband.

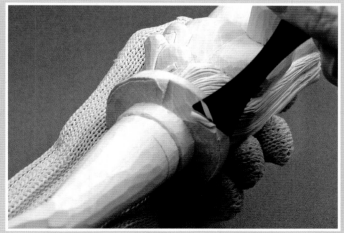

87 Starting ⅛" from the bottom of the brim, carve at an angle up to the hatband with the #3 ⅞" or #3 ⅝" gouge, as shown. This will refine the hat brim. Use carpenter's wood filler to fill any unintended carve marks and to blend the seam lines on the arms and hat.

88 Use a band saw or a scroll saw to cut out the crow pattern from ¾" stock.

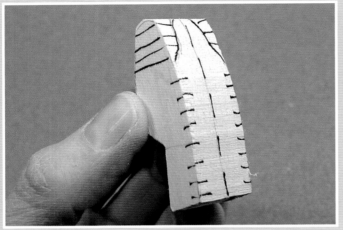

89 Transfer the crow pattern to the back of the wood. The wood in the shaded area will be removed to shape the head and the back.

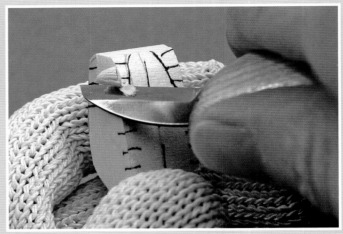

90 Use the bench knife to shape the head.

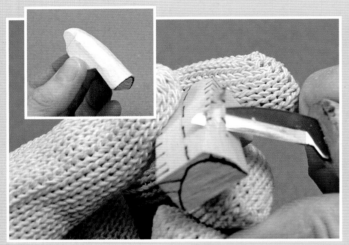

91 Use the bench knife to shape the crow's back.

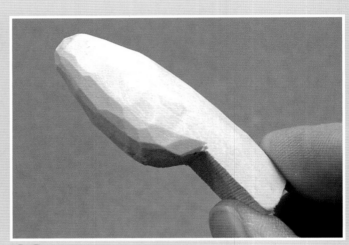

92 Round the edges to define the crow's breast.

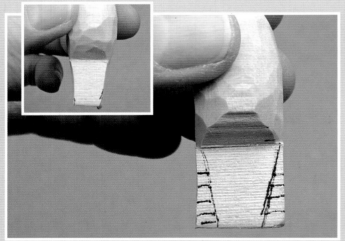

93 Remove the wood in the shaded area of the tail to refine the tail. Carve off any saw marks underneath the tail.

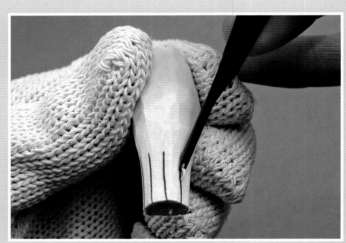

94 Use the 1 mm V-tool to add detail to the tail.

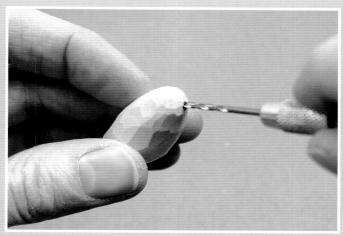

95 Using a hand drill and a 1/16" drill bit, drill a shallow hole in the crow's head, as shown.

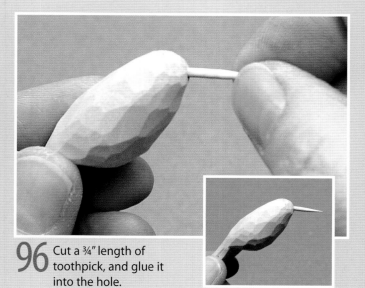

96 Cut a 3/4" length of toothpick, and glue it into the hole.

97 The witch is now ready to be painted.

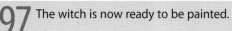

Carving a Crooked Hat

To give your witch a bit of a different look, try this crooked hat instead of the straight one shown in the main demonstration. The steps are slightly more complicated than those for the straight hat, but once you feel comfortable with the techniques, you should have no trouble making either hat.

1 Transfer the crooked hat pattern to the wood. The wood in the shaded area will be removed.

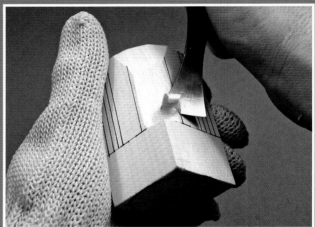

2 Using the #3 ⅞" or #3 ⅝" gouge, remove the wood on the lower portion of the block to form a cylinder.

3 The wood in the shaded area will be removed to form the top of the hat. Note: Wood is not removed all the way around in order to accommodate the kink in the hat.

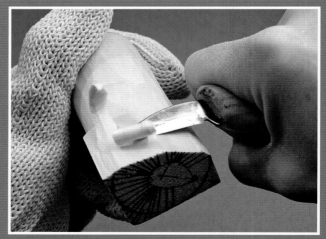

4 Use the bench knife to remove the wood on the top portion of the block and blend it up to the hat pattern on the top of the block, as shown.

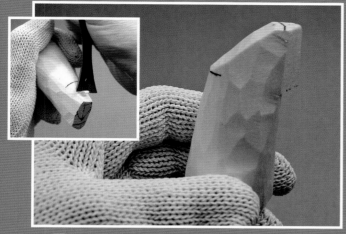

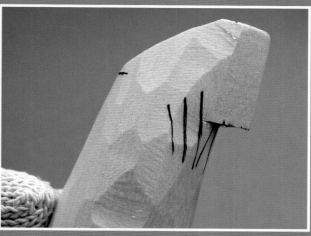

5 Measure down 1" from the top of the block, as shown, and carve a severe slant using the #3 ⅞" or #3 ⅝" gouge. Carve from this line to the dot on the top of the block.

6 Carve in toward the center in the shaded area towards the opposite side using the bench knife.

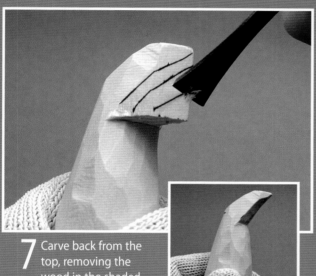

7 Carve back from the top, removing the wood in the shaded area, to define the crooked point using the bench knife.

8 With the bench knife, refine and blend to complete the crooked hat.

Carving the Quilt

Try carving a quilt for your witch to hold instead of the wand and the crow. You'll need to carve two appropriate hands to hold the quilt in addition to carving the quilt itself. Carve a right hand and a left hand using the hand pattern A; then, move on to carving the quilt as described in this section.

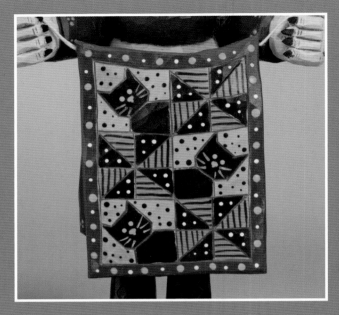

tools and supplies

carving
- ⅜" x 3" x 4" basswood block
- Four 1½" lengths of 20 lb. hemp cord

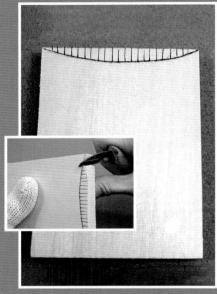

1 Transfer the quilt top pattern to the block of wood. Then, use the bench knife or the #3 ⅞" or #3 ⅝" gouge to remove the wood in the shaded area.

2 Use the #3 ⅞" or #3 ⅝" gouge to round the diagonal corners on the front of the quilt to ⅛" thick.

3 Round the diagonal corners in the shaded areas on the back of the quilt with the #3 ⅞" or the #3 ⅝" gouge.

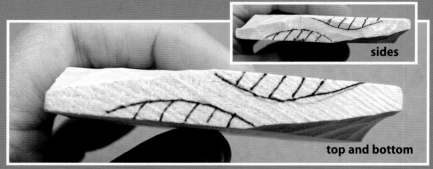

sides

top and bottom

4 Draw the pattern on the top quilt edge, on the bottom quilt edge, and on each side.

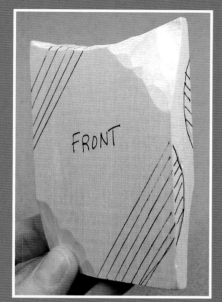

5 The wood in the shaded area on the quilt front will be removed.

6 Use the #9 10 mm gouge to shape the quilt front.

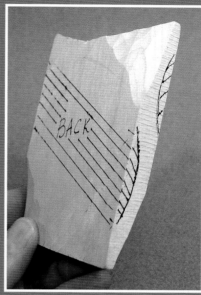

7 The wood in the shaded area on the quilt back will be removed.

8 Use the #9 10 mm gouge to shape the quilt back.

9 Continue to shape the quilt by removing wood on the quilt back. Use the pattern on the top edge of the quilt to see where wood is to be removed.

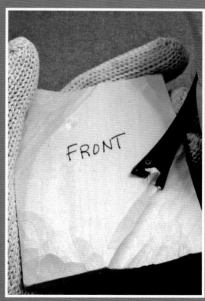

10 Use the #3 ⅞" gouge to evenly blend the quilt front.

Carving the Quilt *(continued)*

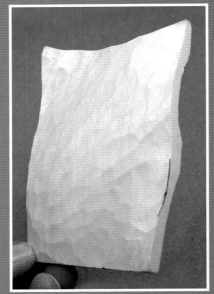

11 Make sure the front is evenly curved without any deep grooves.

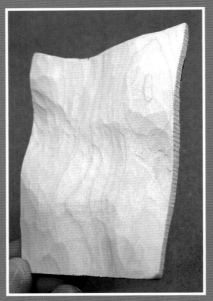

12 Using the #9 10 mm gouge and the #3 ⅞" or the #3 ⅝" gouge, blend the back of the quilt in a similar manner.

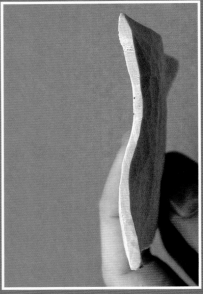

13 Make sure the edges of the quilt are uniformly ⅛" thick. A view of the top quilt edge shows the progress to this point.

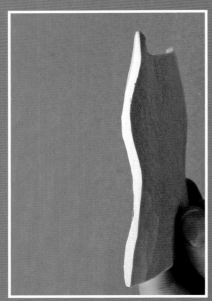

14 This is how the side quilt edge should now look.

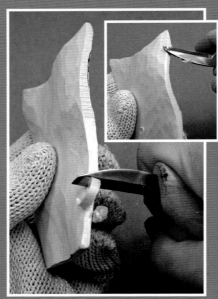

15 Carve off any saw marks that remain on the edges of the quilt with the bench knife. Then, round all the edges of the quilt slightly using the detail knife.

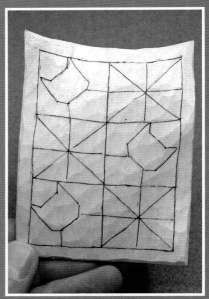

16 Transfer the block pattern to the quilt.

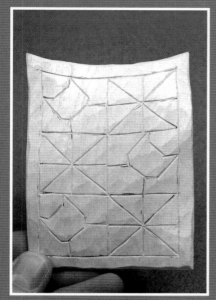

17 Use the 1 mm V-tool to outline the block pattern.

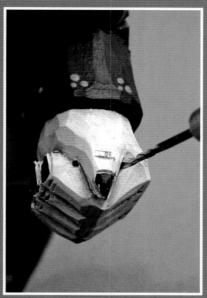

18 After you have painted and finished your witch (see page 106), use the hand drill and the 1/16" drill bit to drill holes 1/4" deep on each side of the witch's thumbs.

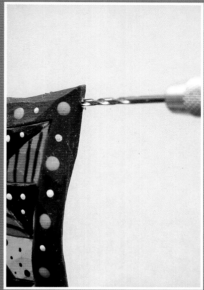

19 Very carefully drill holes in each side of the quilt near the top edge. The wood is very narrow here, and care should be taken to avoid splitting the wood.

20 Tie a knot in one end of two of the 1½" lengths of 20 lb. hemp cord. Add a dot of cyanoacrylate glue to the unknotted ends and insert them in the holes on the outside of the witch's thumbs, as shown.

21 Attach one of the remaining lengths of hemp cord on each side of the quilt using the holes drilled and a dot of cyanoacrylate glue. Position the quilt between the witch's hands and trim each cord to extend 1/4" beyond the hole drilled on the inside of each thumb. Trim away the excess cord.

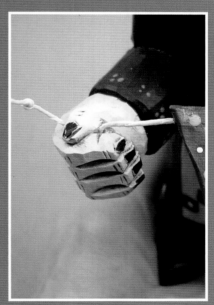

22 Apply a dot of cyanoacrylate glue to the remaining ends of the hemp cord and insert them into the holes on the insides of the thumbs. Allow them to dry.

Painting and finishing

Paint the witch. Proceed with painting the eyes, antiquing, and varnishing the witch. Then, attach the legs, the wand, and the crow.

COLOR CHART

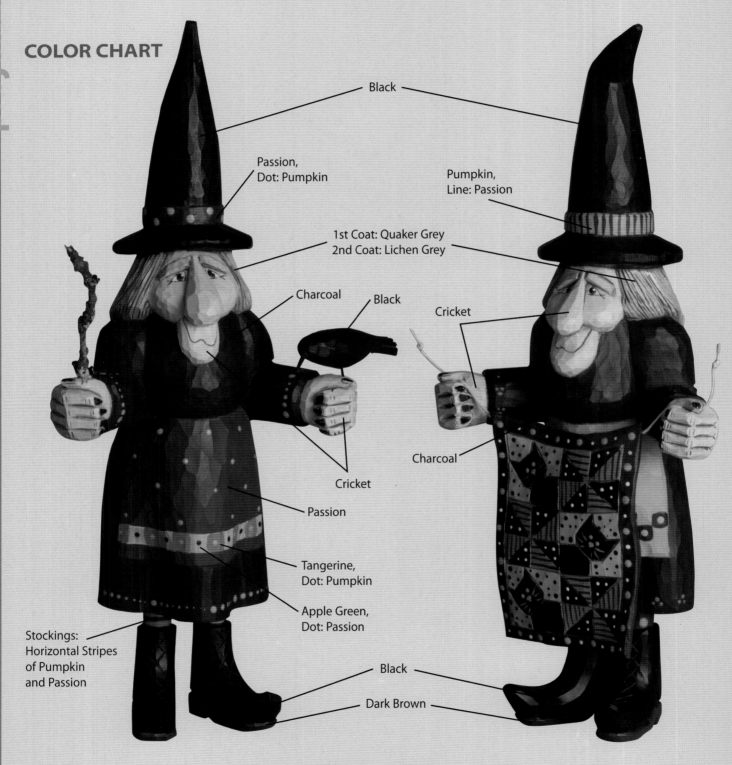

Black

Passion,
Dot: Pumpkin

Pumpkin,
Line: Passion

1st Coat: Quaker Grey
2nd Coat: Lichen Grey

Charcoal

Black

Cricket

Passion

Cricket

Charcoal

Stockings:
Horizontal Stripes
of Pumpkin
and Passion

Tangerine,
Dot: Pumpkin

Apple Green,
Dot: Passion

Black

Dark Brown

Witch is antiqued with one part
burnt sienna, one part raw sienna,
and two parts antiquing medium.

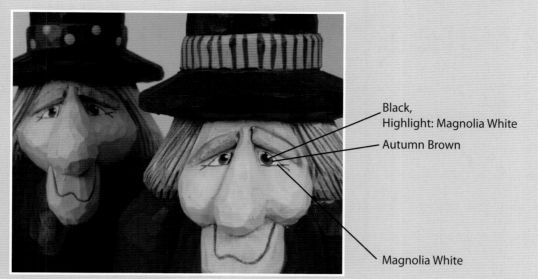

Black,
Highlight: Magnolia White

Autumn Brown

Magnolia White

Line Eyes with Black Extrafine-Line
Permanent Marker

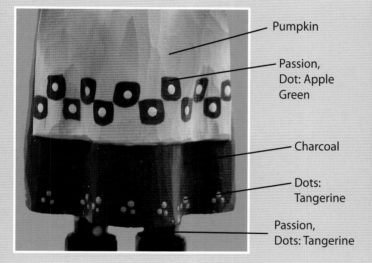

Pumpkin

Passion,
Dot: Apple
Green

Charcoal

Dots:
Tangerine

Passion,
Dots: Tangerine

Passion,
Large Dot: Pumpkin,
Small Dot: Light Ivory

Black,
Dot: Light Ivory

Green Apple,
Dot: Black

Eyes: Green Apple

Nose: Pumpkin

Whiskers: Light Ivory

Tangerine,
Line: Black

1 Paint the eyes. The painting process for the witch's eyes is
the same as for the ghost (see page 79), except that the
whites of the eyes are triangular in shape rather than oval.
This shape makes it appear as if the top lid is a bit droopy.
I also line the eyes with a black extrafine-line permanent
marker to add more definition to the eye.

2 Wire dowel the wand and the crow to the hands
(see page 35).

project 6 beware sign

This is the first of two additional projects I've included in this book. Give them a try once you have completed the rest of the step-by-step projects so that you can use the skills you've learned by finishing the other projects. The Beware Sign is a great project to practice carving in relief. I've included the materials list and some project notes to get you started.

tools and supplies

carving
- 1" x 8" x 20" basswood board for sign
- Bench knife
- Detail knife
- #3 5mm or #3 ⅝" gouge
- Large self-leveling picture hanger

painting
- Acrylic paint, such as Delta Ceramcoat, in the following colors:
  - Apple green
  - Black
  - Blue velvet
  - Charcoal
  - Magnolia white
  - Pumpkin
  - Purple
  - Raw sienna
  - Violet pearl
- Flat brushes in sizes 2 to 8 for blocking color
- #0 or #1 liner brushes for detail painting

varnishing
- Water-based satin-finish varnish, mixed one part water to one part varnish (see page 17)
- ¾" wash brush or small flat brush for smaller parts

antiquing
- Antiquing medium and retarder mixture, such as Jo Sonja's, mixed one part antiquing medium to one part dark flesh acrylic paint (see page 32)
- Old flat brush
- Soft cloth or old T-shirt
- Cotton swabs

Carving notes

• Be very precise in transferring the pattern to ensure that the borderlines and blocks are straight, even, and square.

• Use a bench knife to score all of the straight lines, carving thin wedges from both sides of each line to define the pattern. Round the edges of the sign.

• Use a detail knife to outline the letters.

• Remove a small amount of wood around the letters and between the letters and the border with a #3 ⅝" gouge and a #3 5mm gouge for small and tight areas. Some elements on the letters are very thin, so care should be taken when removing wood around them.

enlarge pattern 200%

Painting and finishing

Paint the sign according to the color chart. Then, varnish and antique the sign (See pages 31–32). Add a large self-leveling picture hanger to the back to finish.

COLOR CHART

Black   Magnolia White   Charcoal   Pumpkin   Purple   Raw Sienna

Apple Green   Blue Velvet - first coat
Violet Pearl - second coat

Beware sign is antiqued with one part
dark flesh and one part antiquing medium.

project 7 halloween candy bowl

For this project, I combined simple relief carved tiles to create a Halloween candy bowl to serve sweets to visiting trick-or-treaters. Not just perfect for decorating the bowl, the tiles are very versatile and can be used for a variety of projects. They would be great for creating pins; you could also enlarge them to create coasters, or you could use them to decorate picture frames or any number of items. Just use your imagination, and there's no limit to what you can create.

Note: This bowl is for decorative use only. It holds wrapped Halloween candy wonderfully. It is not, however, intended for direct contact with any unwrapped food. A bowl with a fairly large circumference is recommended. I used a 15" turned, unfinished bowl (Hofcraft HBM-15, *www.hofcraft.com*).

tools and supplies

carving
- 1¼" x 1¼" x ⅜" basswood tiles
- 15" unfinished turned bowl, such as a Hofcraft HBM-15
- 1 mm V-tool
- Detail knife
- #3 ⅝" gouge, optional
- Zots clear adhesive dots
- Beacon "Quick Grip" All-Purpose Permanent Adhesive

painting
- Acrylic paint, such as Delta Ceramcoat, in the following colors:

Apple green	Black
Charcoal	Ivory
Jubilee green	Light ivory
Opaque yellow	Passion
Pumpkin	Purple
Tangerine	

- Flat brushes in sizes 2 to 8 for blocking color
- #0 or #1 liner brushes for detail painting
- Krylon Silver Leafing Pen

varnishing
- Water-based satin-finish varnish, mixed one part water to one part varnish (see page 31)
- ¾" wash brush or small flat brush for smaller parts

antiquing
- Antiquing retarder, such as Jo Sonja's
- Acrylic paint, such as Delta Ceramcoat - Dark Flesh
- Old flat brush
- Soft cloth or old T-shirt
- Cotton swabs

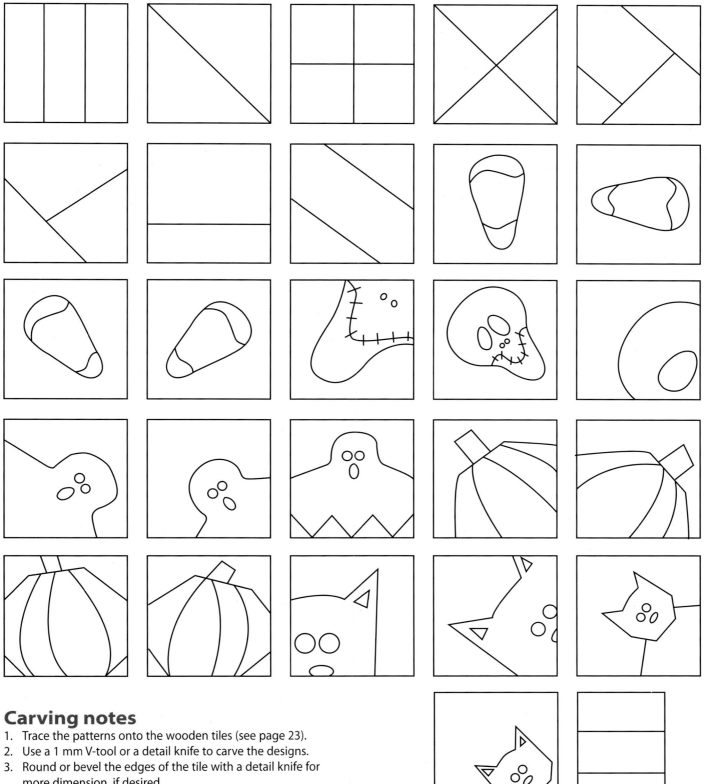

Carving notes

1. Trace the patterns onto the wooden tiles (see page 23).
2. Use a 1 mm V-tool or a detail knife to carve the designs.
3. Round or bevel the edges of the tile with a detail knife for more dimension, if desired.
4. The relief carved tiles are now ready to be painted and assembled onto the bowl.

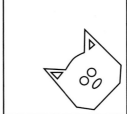

Assembly directions

1. Measure or dry fit the tiles to ensure that you have enough tiles to line the top edge of the bowl. Note: The size of your bowl will determine the number you need. This bowl required 37 tiles.
2. Round the backs of the wooden tiles to fit the contour of the bowl. I used a #3 ⅝" gouge to slightly contour the underside of each tile.
3. Dry fit the carved tiles to the bowl using an adhesive dot. This dot allows you to temporarily adhere the tiles to the bowl to check the fit and spacing. Because I was individually fitting each tile to the bowl's surface as well as to the tiles around it, I numbered the backs of the tiles so I could reassemble them in the same order after they were painted.
4. After the tiles have been fitted to the bowl, remove them for painting.
5. Paint the tiles per directions on page 30.
6. Add painted details.
7. When the paint is completely dry, apply two coats of a water-based varnish (see page 31).
8. Paint the bowl with the colors of your choice or choose from the list on page 112. I used three coats of varnish on the inside and outside of the bowl and added eyes to the inside surface. I did not antique the bowl.
9. Allow the varnish on the tiles and the bowl to dry thoroughly.
10. Permanently adhere the tiles to the outside edge of the bowl using Beacon Quick Grip All-Purpose Permanent Adhesive.
11. Color the rim of the bowl silver with a Krylon Silver Leafing Pen.

COLOR CHART

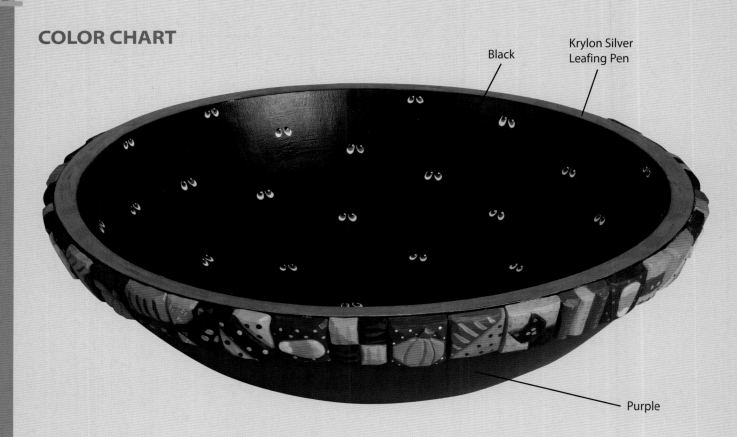

Black

Krylon Silver Leafing Pen

Purple

Tangerine

Opaque
Yellow

Ivory

Pumpkin

Black

Pumpkin

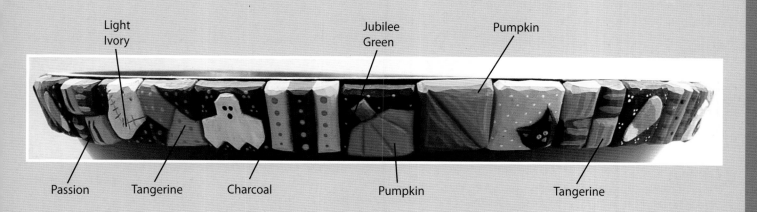

Light
Ivory

Jubilee
Green

Pumpkin

Passion

Tangerine

Charcoal

Pumpkin

Tangerine

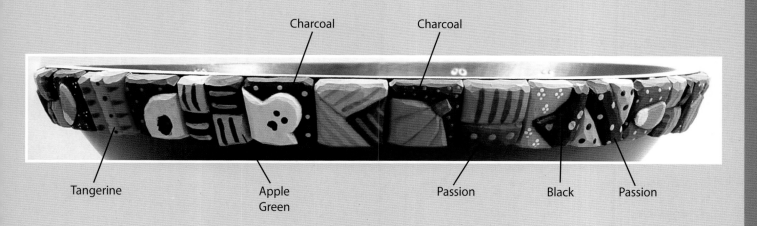

Charcoal

Charcoal

Tangerine

Apple
Green

Passion

Black

Passion

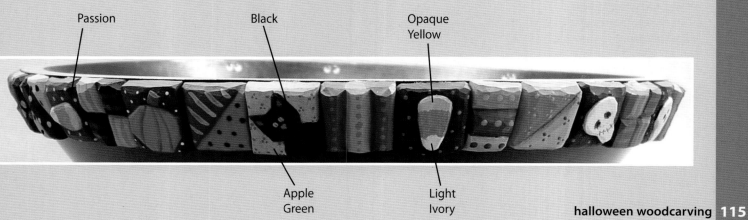

Passion

Black

Opaque
Yellow

Apple
Green

Light
Ivory

resources

Woodcarving clubs

If you don't know where to find a woodcarving club in your area, an excellent source is: *www.woodburning.com*. When the Web site opens, click on "carving clubs."

Carving magazines

Woodcarving Illustrated (*www.woodcarvingillustrated.com*)
Carving Magazine (*www.carvingmagazine.com*)
Chip Chats (*www.chipchats.org*)

Books

Browse catalogs on *www.foxchapelpublishing.com* and you should find woodcarving subjects of interest to you. The authors will each have their own styles and techniques; study and learn how and why they make certain cuts, which tools they use and why they use one tool over another.

Catalogs

If you don't have a source for carving supplies in your area, there are some good catalogs available from which you can order your carving supplies. Any of these suppliers will send you a free catalog if you contact them. Also, try searching the Internet for online suppliers.

The Woodcraft Shop (800-397-2278)
Wood Carvers Supply (800-284-6229)
Woodcraft (800-225-1153)
Klingspor's Woodworking Shop (800-228-0000)
Chipping Away (519-743-9008)
Lee Valley (1-800-871-8158)

Name brand tools.

Some of the most common woodworking tool makers are listed below by tool.

Carving Knives:

Cape Forge, Denny, Flexcut, Helvie, Murphy, Stubai

Chip Carving Knives

Flexcut, Lampbrand, Moor, Pheil, Stubai, Wayne Barton

Chisels / Gouges / "V" Tools

Ashley Iles, Dastra, Denny, Flexcut, Henry Taylor, Lamp Brand, Pheil, Ramelson, Stubai, Swiss Made, Two Cherries, Warren

Micro Tools

Dockyard, Flexcut, Ramelson, Two Cherries

gallery

These pieces are variations on the projects presented in this book. A large palette of colors combined with the ability to mix-and-match elements from different projects will allow you to create an unlimited amount of frightfully fun Halloween pieces. Be creative!

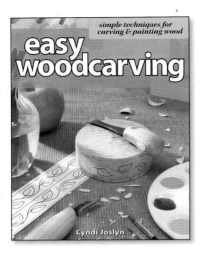

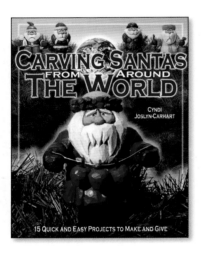
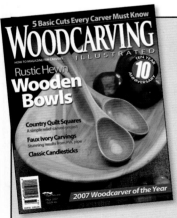